The
CEO's
Advantage

7 Keys for
Hiring Extraordinary Leaders

A LEADER'S STORY

STEPHEN C. MOULTON

Foreword by Don Hutton, FACHE

FLATIRONS
PUBLISHING

Action Interviewing®, Action Coaching®, and ActionPlus® are registered trademarks of Action Insight, Inc.

Designed by: Nick Zelinger

Library of Congress Cataloging-in-Publication Data

Moulton, Stephen, 1952-
  The CEO's Advantage: 7 Keys for Hiring Extraordinary Leaders /
Stephen Moulton.- 1st ed.
  Hardcover ISBN 978-0-9817867-0-4
  Softcover ISBN 978-0-9817867-1-1
  1. Leadership. 2. Executives – Recruiting. 3. Employee Selection
  HF5549.5.R44 2009
  658.4'0711-ddc22
  LCCN: 2008928952

Printed in the United States of America

Requests for permission to make copies of any part of this work can be made to:

FLATIRONS PUBLISHING

Flatirons Publishing.
430 Columbine Avenue
Broomfield, Colorado 80020
1.303.439.2001

CONTENTS

FOREWORD

EVERYONE WHO HAS BEEN a CEO has experienced that disappointment of a new executive not meeting the expectations for them when they were recruited and hired. All the references checked out, the background seemed perfect, the chemistry felt good, everyone who met them thought they were a good fit and yet, after a year, they were struggling and the organization was frustrated with their performance. What went wrong? How could we have made such a poor selection? What were we thinking?

Hiring mistakes are costly not only in cash but in loss of momentum and disruption of the organization.

It is widely known and understood that a CEO's most important task is to select the right people for their executive team. An organization's success is 90% dependent on the ability of the people within that organization to execute.

Top executives are the drivers in the organization. Having great strategies, facilities, technology, or visions is not enough. Execution separates the top performing organizations from the average organization and execution is wholly dependent on having the right people on your team.

This book is a wonderful owner's manual on how to use behavioral competencies in the recruitment and hiring process. This book shows us how to use these behavioral competencies to aid in our success in selecting the right people for the right positions. It shows us the process that needs to be put in place during the recruiting of executive team members.

Moulton's warning about how personal bias can be a powerful influencer on the hiring process is an important concept often overlooked by many organizations and CEOs. These biases prevent us from seeing people and things clearly and often have an undue influence on our judgments and decisions.

They create blind spots that can cause us to take costly missteps in the hiring process. Often the obvious is overlooked due to these blind spots. Using this process can reduce the risk of letting our biases get in our way during the recruiting and hiring process.

This book goes a long way in helping CEOs understand how to reduce the hiring failure rate and more importantly teaches us how we can use the hiring process to make our team more effective. The principles are so simple one would wonder why we did not discover this long ago. Like so many breakthrough strategies we find they are not complex but are made up of simple and straightforward concepts.

This book is a must-read for all CEOs and their executive teams. It will put them on the path to recruiting and hiring the executives they need and want.

Donald H, Hutton, FACHE
President and CEO
Morgan Executive Development Institute (MEDI)

INTRODUCTION

MANY SENIOR LEADERS HAVE had enough success in their careers to believe that they are good judges of character and make excellent hiring decisions. Thinking about this phenomenon, if there is a senior leader in the healthcare industry who has made hiring decisions over at least a ten year period of time and have:

1. hired the right person every time;
2. had the right people in the right positions, and;
3. achieved or even exceeded goals,

call me toll free at 866-439-2001. I want to hear your story and how you have done it.

Why is this important? Leaders have the potential for the biggest impact, either positive or negative.

For instance, consider:

- A healthcare leader who fails to build relationships with doctors, who in turn feel unvalued and eventually take their patients to other hospitals.
- A healthcare leader who turns a failing hospital with patient satisfaction levels in the bottom 10% to a successful hospital with patient satisfaction levels in the top 10%.
- A leader who has turnover of greater than 25% compared to one with less than 10%.

Then there are leaders who:

- Will not go into the organization and talk with employees.
- Do not lead and who find reasons for not coaching and developing their employees, let alone talking to them.
- Micromanage or disempower their employees by doing such things as going around their subordinate managers or even superseding their decisions.
- Punish subordinates if they disagree with a firmly held feeling or belief, even if they are wrong.
- Demonstrate the belief that they have arrived and are above the rules.

Having the right leaders in the right seats at the table is crucial. The ability to predict a candidate's potential for success with certainty is key to success.

In an old W.C. Fields movie, *My Little Chickadee*, a young greenhorn wants to play cards with sharpie W.C. Fields.

> Greenhorn: "Is this a game of chance?"
> W.C. Fields: "Not the way I play it, no."

Stacking the deck in your favor is what this book is about. Hiring leaders should not be treated like a game of chance.

Too often, leaders let candidates generalize and share platitudes about what they have done, thinking they are getting a good feel for the candidate. Frankly, that is bull.

Knowing how to get verifiable information from a candidate that provides you with the ability to predict whether or not the candidate will be successful is important.

Hiring leaders who will be a good fit for the culture and style of the organization can make the difference between success or failure. If the culture is a good one, fit could be critical.

Hiring leaders who can make the cultural or organizational corrections critical for an organization's survival may be essential.

The tragedy is that many leaders intuitively understand the need for this but, lacking alternatives, they struggle with making the necessary changes. Instead they allow first impressions and gut feelings to take the place of a rigorous selection process.

The key to building a great team is in hiring the right people for the right positions in the first place.

Just a note: The time frame in this story is condensed to keep the story moving, and is probably an unrealistic time frame to fill key positions.

CHAPTER 1

Bob Paul

BOB PAUL SAT STARING out his office window, angry and frustrated. He watched icy rain falling in sheets from clouds that were as dark as his disposition.

I've been the CEO of Community Hospital for less than a year, and to have this happen. . .

He sighed, shook his head in disbelief, and brought himself out of his musing.

How could everything have gone so wrong? How could he have been so wrong in his selection of these two key staff members? And now they were both gone.

He looked over at the clock on his desk and saw that it was 4:54 p.m.

Losing two key team members was going to cause turmoil and set his plans back for months. Yet neither of them seemed to have fit in with the staff.

Bob's mind wandered back over the last few weeks. Roger, who had been his Chief Operating Officer for less than six months, had

1

suddenly resigned. *Probably because the Chief Medical Officer and many doctors were up in arms and after his head,* he thought.

Then Marilyn, his Chief Financial Officer, had broken his trust by leaking bid information for the new addition to one of the vendors competing for the contract.

Bob Paul felt the weight of leadership on his shoulders. He certainly was not new to leadership. He had been in the healthcare field for eighteen years and this was not his first position as CEO. But the political nuances of this hospital were different than anything he had previously experienced and he was feeling the pressure of it. To lose two key players did not help.

The phone rang, shattering the silence.

He picked up the phone.

"Bob, Martha Payton is on line one, and she's on the warpath," warned his assistant, Ann.

"Thanks, Ann."

I don't need this now, he thought as he reached to punch line one.

Martha was a board member who had voted against hiring him. He was unsure why, though he believed there had been another candidate she had preferred over him. Bob had hoped his thoughtful way of approaching issues, energetic style, friendly manner, and innate intelligence would eventually win her over. But months had passed and Martha seemed as distrustful and antagonistic towards him as she had been on his first day.

"Good afternoon, Martha, what can I do for you?"

CHAPTER

Martha Payton

"DON'T GOOD AFTERNOON ME, Bob," Martha barked. "What are you doing to my hospital?"

Bob wasn't in the mood for this, but bit his tongue and remained cordial.

"I'm sorry Martha, what are you talking about?"

"Don't play coy with me Bob. I'm talking about how two key team members who report to you have given Community Hospital a black eye with a bid scandal and their leaving in the middle of a growth initiative the board has agreed to fund."

Bob was surprised with the frankness of Martha's confrontation.

"I don't think you need to worry. We will be on track as soon as I can get these people replaced."

"Don't try and placate me; I'm more than upset. Did you hire the CFO?"

Bob nodded to himself as he admitted making the decision.

"Then her failure is your responsibility."

Now Bob's blood pressure went up a bit.

"Did you look into her integrity and management skills when you hired her?"

Bob stammered. "We . . . well, sure . . . I mean, as much as you do with anyone. I mean, I figured she could be trusted if she's at the executive level. She came highly recommended."

Martha persisted. "What are you looking for in her replacement? How are you going to make sure you don't make the same mistake?" Bob couldn't really answer the question.

"What about replacing Roger? Not only didn't he fit in at Community Hospital, but he bailed on you in less than six months after having half of the Docs up in arms."

Martha was pushing all of Bob's buttons and he was way past being agitated with her.

"Look Martha, building my leadership team is my responsibility and it will get my full attention in the next few weeks."

"It had better, Bob, because we have nine weeks before our next board meeting and if I don't see a big change, I will be pushing for more changes."

"Are you threatening me Martha?"

"Let's put it this way, I've read that the failure rate of new CEOs is fifty to sixty percent within their first six years, and you're not off to a very good start Bob."

Martha abruptly hung up.

Board members can be such a pain, Bob thought to himself. But, she is right. I need to get my act together and get some great people in here.

Bob reached for the phone, then glanced at the clock and realized it was well after five o'clock. He got up to leave. As he opened his office door, the quietness of the outer office was stunning.

He walked back to his desk and pulled his calendar up to see what his schedule looked like for the evening.

Leadership Conference 6:00 p.m.
Convention Center

Nuts, he thought, *I promised to introduce William Marks at the Leadership Conference tonight. I'm not really in the mood for this, but it will be great to see William again.*

CHAPTER 3

William Marks

BOB WENT TO THE restroom to splash some water on his face, comb his hair, and straighten his tie. Then he went back to his office to collect his briefcase and slowly walked to the parking lot, feeling the pressure of the position he was in.

I have less than nine weeks before I need to be back on track, he thought as he drove to the new convention center.

As he drove into the parking lot, he looked up at the marquee.

Leadership Conference
William Marks
Key Leadership Secrets Everyone Should Know

That's great, he thought, *maybe I'll pick up a new idea.*

This was a local Chamber of Commerce event and from the number of cars in the parking lot, it seemed to be drawing a large number of business people.

The first thing Bob did after collecting his name tag was get a ginger ale. Taking a deep breath, he scanned the room. He really didn't want to run into Martha and continue that conversation. Luckily, she had not arrived yet. He did see a group with Diane Phillips, his Human Resource Vice President, and moved to join that conversation.

Diane reached out to invite Bob into the group.

"Good evening Bob."

"Good evening everyone. What is the topic of discussion?"

"We were just talking about William Marks," said Diane. "We understand he is an old friend of yours."

"Yes, William and I were roommates in college," Bob explained. "He was a leader then and has been very successful in a number of key positions. I'm looking forward to introducing him tonight."

Just then, Bob spotted William and waved him over to the group.

"William, I would like to introduce you to a few of my friends. This is Diane Phillips, Ann Taylor, John Stevens, and Vicki Garcia. They all work at Community Hospital. Everyone, this is William Marks."

They shook hands.

The Chamber's president interrupted the conversation, ringing an oversized cowbell to get everyone's attention.

"Please take your seats and we will begin the program. I would like to introduce Bob Paul, the President and CEO of Community Hospital, who will introduce our honored guest."

Bob made his way to the podium.

"It is my pleasure to introduce a good friend of mine. William Marks and I went to school together many years ago, he has been a mentor to me as my career has progressed, and we have collaborated on a number of projects.

"Recently, William was tapped to be the Chief Operating Officer of the Community Hospital System. In his last assignment, he was able to turn a struggling hospital around and, after only three years, that hospital won an award as the 'Best Company to Work For' in the state.

"William, please come forward and take a few minutes to share with us the secret of your success."

CHAPTER

Insights

WILLIAM MARKS STRODE CONFIDENTLY to the podium. He was a tall and slender man with a distinguished air about him and a twinkle in his eye. Purposefully looking out into the crowd of well-wishers, he smiled.

"Thank you for inviting me to speak with you this evening. I was asked to share a few thoughts on what has made me successful. As I thought about it, five things came to mind. All of them have to do with building and none of them can be done in isolation, by one person acting alone."

With that, William clicked a hand-held remote and five items appeared on a large screen to his left.

1. Building a strong team.
2. Building relationships.
3. Building a strong shared vision.
4. Building an engaged and innovative environment.
5. Building trust and leading with integrity.

"All of these are critical to business success and all have been instrumental to my personal success. But tonight, in our short time together, I want to focus on just one of these, building a strong team.

"Most people think of team building as going on a white-water raft trip, taking a personality assessment and sharing the results, playing ball together, or going out for drinks.

"Though these tactics can play a role, the first key to building a strong team is hiring the right team members in the first place."

He paused for effect.

"I want to emphasize how important it is to do more than just a *good* job of selecting team members. Let me ask a question. I'd like a show of hands. How many of you have noticed that it is getting harder and harder to hire great employees?"

Almost every hand in the crowd went up.

Pausing for a moment, he then asked, "And how many of you have noticed that the consequences of not hiring the right people are getting harder and harder to live with?"

Again, almost every hand in the crowd went up and many gave an uncomfortable laugh, including Bob, who felt William was looking straight at him.

"Here's a news flash: The first step in building a great team starts with who you hire.

"Here's another news flash . . . and think about this: Not all candidates are equally qualified or productive as employees.

"Not everyone will fit into your organization's culture.

"Not everyone has had the experiences that build the skills that fit your job requirements."

He paused again and scanned the room slowly, pivoting from left to right.

"One more news flash. Most people treat interviewing as an event, rather than a process. They have an opening, get a résumé, meet the candidate, and BAM! You have an interview.

"I have another question for you. Who is more prepared going into an interview, the candidate or the interviewer?"

"The candidate!" someone yelled from the audience.

"That's usually right," admitted William. "Why is that? Here is my thought. You are busy dealing with and juggling five, ten, twenty, or more priorities. The candidate has only one priority: get the job.

"Think about it." He waited for a moment.

"So what do you need to do? I'm going to give you a quick list of seven things you need to do well."

Again he clicked the remote and the first item came up on the screen:

1. Define the position requirements.

"First, you must clearly define the position requirements. How can you effectively tell that someone is qualified for a job if you don't establish criteria in advance?"

He paused for a moment while everyone began writing, then clicked the remote again.

2. Use a structured job-related interview.

He continued.

"Next, create a structured job-related interview. It is important to use the same questions for each candidate interviewing for a position."

Again, he paused, allowing the audience to absorb what he had just said and take notes.

He brought up the third item on the screen.

3. Use past event interview questions.

"Third, use past event interview questions. These are questions that ask the candidate to share an example of a time when they have actually demonstrated a specific behavior. Past actions are the best predictor of future actions. That is so important, I will repeat it. Past actions are the best predictor of future actions."

After another brief pause he continued, bringing the fourth item up on the screen as he spoke.

4. Use a panel or team interview.

"Use a panel or team interview—two to three people, no more—each participating in the interview at the same time. Some people resist this, but there are lots of benefits."

He waited and slowly scanned the room before moving on to the fifth point.

5. Control your biases and first impressions.

"This is a hard one," he admitted. "But if you don't control your biases and first impressions, you risk hiring the wrong person for the job and missing out on the person who might be a perfect fit."

He caught Bob's gaze, and winked before he continued.

6. Establish rating guides in advance.

"I have heard many leaders say they will know it when they see it, but we wouldn't track our financials that way, so why hire that way? Rating criteria should include one simple question. 'Is this the way I would want things handled in my organization?'"

He paused again, waiting a moment for the note takers.

7. Rate candidates by consensus.

"Keep your interview team together after the interview and rate the candidate's responses against your rating criteria.

"If you will do these seven things well, you can significantly increase the reliability of your selection decisions and get people who better fit your position requirements and the culture of your organization.

"Earlier, I gave you five elements I believe have contributed to my success. It all begins with building a great team. Begin with that and you begin down the road to success.

"Thank you again for inviting me to be a part of this program. I hope you have gained something of value. Now, I'm sure some of you have questions. I would be happy to field them at this time."

A microphone had been placed in the center aisle for those with questions and a long line quickly developed. Clearly, this topic had resonated with many business people in the audience.

Bob was one of them. As William talked, Bob came to a decision. He needed William's help . . . and he was going to ask for it.

CHAPTER

Seeking Insight

THE CROWD OF WELL-WISHERS had slowly thinned from around William and the last person shook his hand and walked away. Bob approached.

"William, great presentation. Your remarks really struck a chord."

"Bob Paul, it's so good to see you. I'm happy you were here and pleased that the presentation was meaningful to you. We didn't have much of a chance to chat before the program. How are you doing?"

"Hanging in there . . . well no, not really, William. I really messed up and I know you are busy with the new job, but I could really use your advice. Could I schedule some time with you? I'd like you to teach me more on your hiring process."

"Sure Bob, I would be happy to. But let's take a few minutes to talk about what's happening. Give me a little time to get my stuff together. Why don't you meet me in the lobby?"

"Thanks William."

Bob walked toward the lobby thinking about what he had heard over the last hour and wondering if there was really a way to tell if someone would be successful in a job before hiring them. If so, he knew he needed to learn more about it and learn it soon.

About fifteen minutes later, William walked into the lobby and found Bob sitting in one of the overstuffed chairs by the front door. Standing, Bob shook his hand and thanked him again for taking the time to talk with him. William smiled and sat in the chair facing Bob.

"Well, Bob, what seems to be the problem?"

"Do you want the long story or the executive summary?"

"Let's start with the executive summary, and I'll ask questions if I need more information."

"I have lost two of my executive team members in the last week."

"Okay, tell me more."

"Well, about a month ago we put out a bid for the new wing of the hospital. Several contractors did the walk-through and one got cozy with Marilyn, my CFO. I found out that last week she shared the final numbers from other bids with that contractor, to give him an advantage."

"What did you do?" William asked, warming up to the story.

"I really felt betrayed, and since she had lost my trust, I let her go."

"You said you lost two of your executive team," William probed.

"Yes, my COO just resigned after less than six months to take a job with another hospital. I didn't see that one coming either. Their references were so good.

"William, I've been hiring staff members for years, and I know a good candidate when I see one. Sure, I've made a few hiring mistakes, but I've also hired some good ones."

"I understand how you feel, Bob. I have found that, as CEOs, we succeed just enough to think we are good at hiring. And yet, too often we fly by the seat of our pants and let our first impressions guide our selection decisions.

"Let me share the results of a study I ran across. It essentially said that the typical interview most people use—I call scratch and sniff interviewing—has a reliability of predicting job success of less than 30%. Think about it, Bob. With a reliability of less than 50%, you might as well flip a coin."

"That's scary, but what do you mean by reliability?" Bob asked.

"Good question. What I mean by reliability is the ability to get consistent, accurate results. After reading about what these researchers found, I began to develop the process I spoke of tonight," William responded.

"William, is it really possible to tell that much difference between candidates, to really determine who will shine and who won't?" Bob was skeptical.

"Well, that's another great question. While I was developing my process, I found another set of researchers who looked at the differences in productivity between the top 10% of producers and the bottom 10% of producers in three different levels of job complexity.

"For instance, in the simplest of jobs, like unskilled labor, what do you think was the percentage difference in productivity between the top producers and the bottom producers?"

"I wouldn't think much, maybe 15%?" Bob responded.

"How about 300%?"

Bob was shocked.

"You're kidding."

"Bob, the middle group was twelve times more productive. Now the jobs of high complexity, your leadership jobs, would fall into this group. The poor producers actually had negative numbers, losses, and the top producers had very high positive numbers. Mathematically, the difference between the two groups is almost infinite."

William continued, noting Bob's interest.

"You need to be able to identify people who have the right competencies and do things in the right way before you make a hiring decision."

"Okay," Bob acquiesced, "I guess I'm in a jam here and really need to get two exceptionally good team members on board and get us back on track fast. Would you have any time in the next couple of days when I could buy you breakfast or lunch and learn more?"

William thought for a moment.

"Sure, Bob, how about tomorrow morning? I promised to have breakfast with an old friend, but as I think about it, she may be able to help. Shall we say 7:30 at the Breakfast Diner?"

"That would be great, William. I'll leave a message for Ann to clear my calendar."

As they got up to leave, Martha Payton walked past.

"Thank you, William, for your presentation," she said, pausing for a moment. "It was enlightening. Nine weeks, Bob."

CHAPTER 6

New Beginning

BOB WAS FEELING PRETTY good as he walked through the door of the Breakfast Diner. He was immediately met by the hostess.

"Good morning Shari. I'm supposed to meet William Marks here this morning."

"Yes, Bob. I seated them in the private dining area. You know where it is."

"Sure do. By the way, who's with William?"

"Martha Payton."

Bob just rolled his eyes. *So Martha is William's old friend.* He was a bit startled at the prospect of having her privy to his conversation with William, but he was determined to see it through and walked back to the private dining area.

"Good morning William, Martha," he said with a pleasantness that surprised even him.

William quickly explained.

"Bob, you know Martha? She and I go way back. We started our careers together at the same hospital in St. Louis, about twenty years ago.

"Martha," he continued, "Bob and I were roommates in college, so we have known one another even longer than you and I have. You could say we cut our teeth together as budding hospital administrators.

"Okay, to save time, as you will recall from last night, the first step is to do a job analysis. One of the jobs you must fill is the Chief Financial Officer, right?"

Bob nodded his head in agreement.

William continued.

"Martha has held that responsibility at another hospital in the past and is an active CPA now, so I thought her insight would be useful in gaining a clear picture of the competencies necessary for your new CFO's success."

Bob thought about it and reluctantly considered that Martha's collaboration might take some of the pressure off.

"Good idea, where do we start?" Bob asked, with as much enthusiasm as he could muster.

"First, Bob, let me reiterate a couple of things I mentioned last night in my talk. Most candidates are more prepared than the interviewers. That is because most interviewers treat interviewing as an event rather than a process. Remember W. Edwards Deming?"

"Yes," responded Bob.

"He said that 94% of failures are the result of not using a time-tested process."

William paused just long enough for the statistic to sink in.

"What I'm about to share with you is a time-tested process, a process that will stack the deck in your favor and make it much easier to make solid hiring decisions.

"One thing, though. You must promise that once I have shared this process with you, you will share it with other leaders. Agreed?"

"Agreed," said Bob.

"Okay, Bob. Remember, last night I shared that the first step is to conduct a job analysis?" William asked.

Bob nodded his head.

"The first thing we need to do is identify the essential competencies necessary for success.

"To start with, there are two basic kinds of competencies you can hire people for: technical competencies and behavioral competencies.

"Technical competencies are the competencies people learn in school, at workshops, or on the job. They are usually easy to learn and can be learned over a relatively short period of time."

Martha jumped in.

"So technical competencies for a CFO are learned in a college accounting program and then refined based on job experiences."

"Yes," confirmed William, "but they are only one dimension of the profile."

He continued.

"Behavioral competencies, on the other hand, are the work habits and the way people go about getting things done. These are hard to learn and include competencies such as: self-control, responsiveness, collaboration, and integrity.

"What we are going to focus on in the next half an hour is how to identify the top eight competencies for the CFO job. But we are going to do it in a structured manner. I'm going to read a series of behaviors and the two of you are going to come to consensus on a rating.

"Here are your choices: a one will mean that it is seldom or never needed for the job; a two will mean that it is sometimes important for the job; a three will mean that it is important for the job, and; a four will mean that it is very important for the job, so critical that if someone doesn't exercise this well, they would probably get fired."

"You mean something like Marilyn's sharing sensitive information?" asked Bob.

"Precisely," responded William. "Are you two ready?"

Both nodded their heads.

"Now everything can't be very important, so I am going to challenge you to limit the number of threes and fours as we go. We have 96 of these to rate.

"Okay let's start. To what extent does this position require the job holder to handle frequent job changes or unexpected disruptions?"

Bob started. "I think that would be a . . . two."

Martha agreed.

"Okay," said William. All of the questions begin with the same phrase and end with a different behavior."

He read the next behavior. ". . . initiate building cooperative relationships with others?"

Martha jumped in with, "That's a four!"

Bob nodded his head in agreement.

William continued ". . . listen and convey understanding of other's points of view?"

"I rate that a four," said Bob.

"I would rate it a three, maybe, no more," responded Martha.

"Why a three?" Bob asked.

"Because, to William's point, if a CFO didn't 'always' listen and convey understanding of other's points of view, they probably wouldn't get fired."

"Hmmm, I see what you mean," Bob replied.

William read another. ". . . understand the needs of others to influence outcomes?"

"I think that is probably sometimes important but doesn't happen often." Bob replied. "Two?"

Martha agreed.

William read on. ". . . initiate building cooperative relationships with others?"

Martha piped in on this one. "I think this is important. I'd say a three."

Bob nodded his head in agreement.

William continued reading each of the behaviors as Bob and Martha came to agreement on the ratings, completing the analysis in about twenty-five minutes.

"Okay," said William as he finished adding up the rating scores, "here are the top eight competencies."

He wrote them on a piece of paper and slid it between Bob and Martha.

1. Leadership
2. Integrity
3. Trust and Respect

4. Develop Relationships

5. Team Building

6. Strategic Perspective

7. Concern for Quality

8. Collaboration

"That's interesting. I don't think I would have focused on those competencies thirty minutes ago. But I see why they would be important for success in this position," Bob thought out loud.

Then he asked, "Martha? Do you agree with this list of competencies?"

After thinking about it for a moment she responded, "Yes, I can see how knowing how a candidate has demonstrated these in the past would make it possible to predict their fit for the hospital."

"What's next?" asked Bob.

"Wow, look at the time!" Martha exclaimed. "I need to run. William, thanks for including me in this process. Bob, this is good stuff. I'm going to hold you accountable for making sure that the next CFO is able to demonstrate these competencies before you make a hiring decision."

Martha grabbed her notebook and without getting Bob's response, dashed out of the diner.

"I guess that means I'm buying breakfast," Bob laughed.

"Okay, William. We now know what competencies are important for the CFO position, but I don't see how having a list of competencies is going to help me assess a candidate. So, how do I use these to assess a candidate?" asked Bob.

CHAPTER 7

The Structured Interview

"THAT IS A GOOD QUESTION, Bob. But let me ask you a question first. When you make decisions, do you like to gather information so you can compare apples to apples? For instance, let's say you are considering purchasing an expensive piece of hospital equipment. You have two choices. Do you compare features and prices?"

"Well, obviously, I prefer to be able to compare apples to apples," Bob responded. "Using your example, I would compare features, benefits, previous experience with the vendors, and prices. In other words, I would make a fair comparison between the two options."

"That is what a structured interview gives you," replied William. "One research study showed that using a structured interview was more than twice as effective as winging it with an unstructured interview.

"When you have interviewed candidates in the past, have you asked each of the candidates for the same position, the same set of questions?"

"No. That wouldn't be very personal and would stifle candidates," Bob replied, sounding a bit defensive.

"Let me ask you another question. What could be more personal than talking to someone about their experiences?"

"I never thought of it that way. Well, that kind of makes sense," Bob admitted, "but it just doesn't feel right."

"I understand that most executives do not use a rigorous process for selecting a candidate to become a team member. Most prefer the good ole boy process."

William continued. "Let me ask you a question. Do you wing it when it comes to tracking the financial status of your hospital?"

"Of course not! That would be foolish," Bob replied.

"Do you expect the same report format each month?" William asked.

"Of course."

"Why?"

"I need to be able to compare apples to apples! Aha! I get it. Using structure helps me assess each candidate's level of skill and competence against the same criteria, then determine who's qualified, and then compare qualified candidate to qualified candidate."

"Yes, simply speaking, a structured interview is a list of questions that you ask each candidate in the same way each time."

"Okay William, I get it. Now what kinds of questions should I ask?"

CHAPTER 8

The Questions

"BOB, REMEMBER LAST NIGHT I mentioned that the third step is to use past-event interview questions?" William asked.

"Yes?" responded Bob.

"Let's talk for a few minutes about the quality of interview questions in general. Suppose you ask a question like, 'Are you a CPA?' What kind of answer will you get?"

"A *yes* or *no*," replied Bob.

"That's right. How can you know if they really have a CPA license?" asked William.

"I guess you wouldn't unless you followed up and asked for a copy," Bob said without a lot of confidence.

"That's right, Bob. These are called closed-ended questions and closed-ended questions aren't very useful in predicting job success."

William continued. "So let's move on. We have all learned not to ask questions that are often referred to as illegal questions about marital status, child care plans, age, religion, race, and national origin. So I won't spend any more time on those."

"I think I'm pretty clear on that topic," Bob responded.

"Good. The next category of questions often used in interviews is what I call weird or unusual interview questions. Such questions as: Why do we park on driveways and drive on parkways? If you were a tree, what kind of tree would you be? Where does the light go when it goes out? Why are manhole covers round?"

"William, I can see how weird and unusual questions can put a candidate in an uncomfortable position. But isn't that what we need to do, to test a candidate's ability to deal with pressure?" Bob asked.

"I believe an interview should be a professional exchange of information rather than an effort by an interviewer to play junior psychologist," replied William.

"That leads us to another kind of question that is often asked, called a hypothetical question. It would sound like this: What would you do if . . .? How would you handle a situation like . . .? Now Bob, what kinds of responses do you get to hypothetical questions?"

"Hypothetical answers?" Bob answered slowly.

"That's right," William confirmed. "And do you think hypothetical answers are useful in predicting the success of a candidate?"

"Probably not. I guess they would be textbook responses. So what kinds of questions should I ask?"

"Last night I said that the best predictor of future actions is past actions. Do you remember that?"

"Yes, I remember you saying that," Bob replied.

"Well, the best way to do that is to ask questions about a candidate's past experiences that are related to the competencies we have identified," William pointed out.

Bob was a bit confused. "I'm not sure I understand what you mean by questions about a candidate's past experiences."

William continued.

"Questions about past experiences, that can be verified, tell us how a candidate works. We now know what competencies are important and the ratings we did on the behaviors tell us which behaviors are important . . . leading us to which questions are important.

"For instance, one of the leadership behaviors is, 'lead people past the status quo and achieve new levels of excellence.'"

He jotted something on a piece of paper and slid it over to Bob.

Leadership often means disrupting comfort zones in order to lead people past the status quo and achieve new levels of excellence. Describe a time when you were able to do this.

"This is a question that would correspond to that behavior."

The lights went on for Bob.

"I see. Questions about how someone has handled a previous situation can help me predict how they will handle similar future situations."

"When we are done today, I will send you a list of interview questions you can use to assess candidates for these competencies. But having a list of questions is only as good as the interviewer's skills in using them," said William. William paused for a moment to allow his last comment to sink in, then continued.

"Once you have the right questions, it's important to read them exactly as they are written. Don't paraphrase the questions. You need to ask each candidate for a specific position each question the same way, to maintain the integrity of the process."

"That's interesting. So what else do I need to know about using these questions? How hard can it be?" asked Bob, sounding a bit frustrated.

"Let's spend some time on this," William responded.

CHAPTER 9

Using the Questions

"BOB, THE FIRST THING TO remember is that using these questions is a whole different way to interview. So let's talk about what you need to do differently. Here's a question: What does our culture say about maintaining eye contact?"

Bob looked away and thought for a moment.

"If someone doesn't maintain eye contact, they are lying."

"When you were thinking just a moment ago, were you maintaining eye contact?" asked William.

"No, I guess I wasn't."

"So, are you lying?"

"Of course not!"

"That's my point. When we ask questions about past experiences, people will naturally break eye contact as they are thinking about their answer. Even as they are responding, they may break eye contact.

"What is actually happening is that when an individual is asked to share an experience from the past, it is as if they go to the data bank in their brain and look for the file with that information. Then

33

they run a short movie in their mind to freshen the memory so they can share it with you."

"Ah, I get it," Bob responded, thinking out loud.

"Good!" said William.

"You also need to know that people may need some thinking time. So if they struggle a bit, allow them time to think. Don't be in a hurry to jump in and help them. It is important to allow ten to fifteen seconds of silence. That may not sound long, but try it some time. After about ten seconds, you can break the tension by saying something like, 'take your time,' or 'we have plenty of time' and then allow the candidate another ten or so seconds."

"So I'm allowing the candidate a total of twenty seconds?" asked Bob.

"Actually, I would do it twice and allow up to thirty seconds if necessary. Most candidates will usually think of something in the first twenty seconds, but your questions will only pay off if you get an answer."

"Good point." Bob reflected a moment. "I remember this happening with Marilyn. I had asked her a question and I got uncomfortable with the silence when she didn't answer right away. I told her not to worry about it. I had more questions to ask, so I moved on."

"Did you go back to that question before you finished the interview?" William asked.

"No, I didn't want to embarrass her."

"Simply telling the candidate you will return to that question later gives them fair warning. What I have found is that when people struggle with these questions, it is usually early in the interview,"

William offered. "As the interview progresses, it kind of primes the pump and the candidate thinks of more examples that they can share. So, don't forget to return to any skipped questions.

"Remember your questions will only pay off if you get an answer."

"I can see how I need to get answers to my questions, but when I'm interviewing a candidate one-on-one, I can't catch everything."

Bob was beginning to see that he had not done a very good job in his interviews.

CHAPTER 10

Team Interviews

"WILLIAM, BEFORE WE MOVE on to the next key, let me make sure I have the first three right."

"Good idea, Bob."

William was impressed with Bob's interest.

"First, it is important to clearly define the position requirements by doing some sort of job analysis, such as we did.

"Second, create a structured job-related interview from the job analysis. I really liked how you identified those interview questions from the analysis we did. Now I can compare apples to apples.

"Third, use past event interview questions, so I can use past actions to predict future actions."

William was gratified that Bob was serious about the process.

"Terrific, Bob. That leads us to the next key. Have you taken it on yourself to be the sole interviewer and decision maker when it comes to hiring staff members?"

"Yes, why?"

"What do you see as the advantage of doing a single interview?" William asked.

"Well, it's fast and I can make my decision right then."

Bob was wondering where this was leading.

"What do you see as a potential disadvantage to just doing a single interview?"

"Well," Bob replied, then paused to think. "I guess, I'm limiting the decision to just my perception of the candidate."

"That's right," William confirmed.

"So how many people do I need to include when I interview a candidate?" Bob asked.

"Well, here I go with research again," William responded. "I remember one researcher telling me that any more than four interviewers really adds no value to the hiring decision."

"So," Bob thought out loud, "I need to have more than myself as an interviewer, but I don't need any more than four interviewers?"

"That's right," said William. "So let's talk about the team interview."

"Won't a team interview intimidate candidates and make them uncomfortable?" asked Bob.

"Maybe . . ." William paused for a moment, "if you make the interview intimidating, such as having four interviewers on one side of a table and the candidate on the other side. That would make it feel like it was an inquisition."

"I probably wouldn't feel good in that kind of situation either," Bob agreed. "How do I prevent the interview from being intimidating?"

William liked Bob's thoughtfulness.

"Okay, try to create an environment with no barriers between you and the candidate. For instance, you could sit at the end of a conference table, or around a small, round table. But avoid sitting behind a desk."

"Makes sense," Bob replied.

"There are four really good reasons for using a team interview. Can you think of any reasons?" William probed.

"Well," Bob responded, "as team interviewers, we all hear the responses to questions at the same time."

"Very good. Another is that you can synergistically play off each other and probe for more complete information," William offered, and then continued.

"A third really good reason is that when the interview is done, you are all together to rate the candidate's responses.

"And finally—probably one of the most important—note taking duties can be shared. Bob, do you take good notes when you are interviewing?"

"Take good notes?" Bob joked. "Are you kidding? I haven't ever taken notes when I've conducted interviews."

"That's what I thought. You need to take very detailed notes of as much of what the candidate says related to the question as possible. Not only will you better document the interview, but you'll be a better listener."

"Okay," Bob replied. "But I don't see what taking good notes has to do with a team interview."

"Why don't you take notes in an interview?" asked William.

"It would ruin my rapport with the candidate if all I did was write while she was talking."

Bob was confident in his response.

"I can understand that reason. So if you are doing a team interview, you can maintain rapport with the candidate while you ask questions and your team members can take copious notes. Then when *they* are asking questions, you need to take good notes. This is a team effort. Get the idea?"

Bob was nodding his head as he asked his next question. "William, who should I include on my team?"

"Bob, I'd think you would want someone who would be a peer as one team member. For instance, if you are interviewing for your CFO, include Diane Phillips, your VP of Human Resources. If you want a third person, how about Martha Payton?"

Bob had a knee-jerk reaction to the suggestion.

"Martha! Are you kidding? Whose side are you on?"

"Yours, of course. You already have her buy-in on the competencies. Her participation in the interview could build a bridge for future support."

"Yeah, I didn't think about that," Bob admitted.

"Besides, Bob," William added, "having a team will minimize the potential for personal biases that could cloud the final decision."

"Personal biases? What do you mean? I don't have personal biases."

CHAPTER 11

Controlling Biases
and First Impressions

"BOB, ANSWER THIS: WHEN you first met with Marilyn to interview her, at what point did you decide she would be a good candidate?"

"William, come on, I'm really good at reading people and I felt that she would be great within the first five minutes of the interview. She made a great impression. She was sharp."

"So, within just a few minutes you had her sized up?" William asked.

"You bet!" replied Bob.

"You and about 85% of interviewers."

"What?"

Bob was shocked.

"Yep, it seems that several researchers have found that 85% of untrained interviewers react this way," William confided.

"One of the biggest mistakes interviewers make is to decide first

41

and ask questions later. How much information can you get from a candidate in five minutes?"

"I hate to say it," Bob lamented, "but I guess not much."

"You're right. Not much. Many executives make the same mistake, then add to the mistake by doing a brief interview and spending a majority of their time selling the job."

"I never thought of it that way."

Bob wasn't very comfortable learning about all the mistakes he'd made.

"Another mistake is called the halo effect. Are you familiar with the concept?" William asked.

"Yes, that is where I have a bias in favor of the candidate. For instance, I might have something in common with the candidate, such as having graduated from the same college, served in the same branch of the military service, or grown up in the same home town. I assume the candidate is good because he is like me."

"That's right," William replied. "As an interviewer, you need to be careful and avoid such influences. Another cause of candidate error would be stereotyping. Stereotyping can take the form of grouping types of people together based on oversimplified conceptions, opinions, or beliefs about culture, sex, race, or almost anything else."

"I'm struggling with the idea that I've let biases impact my decisions. I have to admit that the thought makes me uncomfortable."

"Well, Bob, when you were impressed with Marilyn, you said she was sharp. What did that mean?"

"She was quick with answers. I felt she was decisive, confident, and smart," said Bob.

"Great, that proves my point. You just said that sharp equals decisive, confident, and smart and you came to that conclusion based on how quick she could provide answers. Yet, you really had no evidence to support your interpretation."

"Ah, I see what you mean."

Bob was beginning to see how easily this could happen.

"I can see how my biases can lead to errors and ultimately become a key reason for my interviewing failures."

"Understanding and dealing with your first impressions and 'gut feelings' is a great step."

"William, I have a question. Are you saying that using my intuition is something I shouldn't be doing at all?"

"That is a good question. I see intuition being used in two aspects of the process. First, use your intuition when you are asking the questions. Rather than assuming you know what a candidate is saying, use your intuition to ask additional questions to gain clarity.

"Second, if you have a couple of qualified candidates who match your requirements, use your intuition to help you make a final decision. The big difference is that you have gathered verifiable information about the candidates and know both are qualified. Make sense?"

Bob could see the wisdom of William's counsel.

"Yes, that makes sense."

"Okay Bob, we have already talked about two ways to minimize error and bias. The first is to use a structured interview and the second is to use a team interview process. Both will help you treat each candidate fairly and equally."

"I can see," Bob admitted, "how a structured interview and team interview can help me keep to the structure and process. But I'm not sure I understand what to do with the candidate's responses once the interview is over."

CHAPTER 12

Rating Guidelines
and Consensus Rating

"THAT IS WHY HAVING established rating guidelines in advance can be so useful. The interview questions I'm giving you are for specific competencies and each competency has a definition.

"For instance, the definition for the Leadership: Able to develop and inspire others to take personal responsibility; get factions with competing perspectives to learn from one another; integrate efforts and talents of team members; lead people past status quo to achieve new levels of excellence.

"Notice there are four components to the definition, four abilities."

He quickly jotted them down for Bob and slid the piece of paper across the table.

1. develop and inspire others to take personal responsibility;
2. get factions with competing perspectives to learn from one another;
3. integrate efforts and talents of team members, and;

4. lead people past status quo to achieve new levels of excellence.

"Okay, I see how it breaks down into four components," said Bob.

"Remember the interview question I shared with you earlier?" asked William.

"Here, let me share it again: 'Leadership often means disrupting comfort zones in order to *lead people past the status quo and achieve new levels of excellence.* Describe a time when you were able to do this.'

"Notice that this question includes the wording used in the fourth component of the definition of leadership."

"Ah, yes, I see that," said Bob, nodding his head.

"You need to use two questions for each competency, to gather information. Then, based on how the candidate describes their experience, you can compare how they went about resolving the issue they faced to the components of the competency you are examining through the question. You should refer back to each of the four behaviors in the definition. Then ask yourself if the candidate's responses addressed any of the four aspects of the definition and whether the way they handled it fits the way you would want it done at Community Hospital. Does this process make sense?"

"Yes, now I see why it is so important to take good notes and do the rating as soon as possible after the interview."

Bob was looking more comfortable.

"Good." William continued. "Your last thought about doing the rating as soon after the interview as possible is important. Your rating of the candidate needs to be done as a team, going through the notes together and coming to consensus on the ratings. I use a very simple rating scale."

William pulled a folder from his briefcase, turned to a grid-lined page, and slid it over to Bob.

Strong evidence the candidate lacks the competency	Some evidence the candidate lacks the competency	Some evidence the candidate has the competency	Strong evidence the candidate has the competency

"I'll send you the sample format."

"That would be good," said Bob, writing feverishly.

William continued.

"Using the competency definition with corresponding questions helps you assess whether or not the candidate possesses the competencies important to you. If the candidate gives examples that address one or two of the behaviors in the definition in a positive way, then there is some evidence that they have the competency.

"On the other hand, if their answers are not a good fit or show they lack the competency, the same rule would apply in the opposite direction."

"What if they address in a positive way three or four of the behaviors?" Bob asked.

"Then there would be strong evidence the candidate has the competency," William said, "and the reverse would be strong evidence that they lack the competency. Before we break, do you think you have the seven keys clearly in your mind?"

"I think so. Let me do a quick review."

Bob wanted to be sure he had it all down. He looked at his notes as he spoke.

"I have:

1. Conduct a job analysis.
2. Create a structured job-related interview.
3. Use past event interview questions.
4. Use a team interview.
5. Control my biases and first impressions.
6. Establish and use rating guides.
7. Rate candidates by consensus.

Did I get them all?"

"You sure did. Bob, we have covered a lot this morning. Now the ball is in your court. Feel free to call me if you have a question."

William rose to leave.

"I'll send over a blank competency analyzer and the interview questions this afternoon."

"Thank you, William. You're a good friend and a great advisor! I really appreciate your time and your coaching. It has really opened my eyes and you may hear from me."

Bob reached for the check.

CHAPTER 13

The Search

AS BOB DROVE BACK to the hospital, he felt his brain was full from the data dump he had received from William. *Well*, he thought, *I wonder what has stacked up for me to deal with while I was gone.*

It had been raining and was cold when Bob left the Breakfast Diner. The rain had stopped but it was still cold as Bob got out of his car. He checked his watch and saw that it was 12:23 p.m. *Good, it's lunchtime and I'll be able to slip into my office.*

At his desk, he began going through his messages. There were only eight, but the one on top was marked "urgent." It was from Albert Carlson, Chairman of the Community Hospital Board of Directors.

Bob picked up the phone and dialed Albert's number. Albert picked up on the second ring.

"This is Al."

Bob would have recognized Al's low, gravelly voice even if he had not identified himself.

"Al, this is Bob Paul. I had a message you called."

"Bob, thanks for calling. I heard from Martha Payton last night that you've lost two of your key executive staff. Is that true?"

"Yes Al, it is true. All in one afternoon. Not a pleasant situation."

"Martha told me she's put you on notice," said Al. "She says she warned you that if you don't have things fixed and on track by the board meeting, she is going to move to replace you. She is really steamed."

"Yes, Martha and I had that conversation, but I didn't realize she was escalating it to you as well."

Bob was fuming, but he bit his tongue, wanting to retain some semblance of professionalism and control.

"Not just me Bob, the whole board. You know she has never really been one of your supporters. You only have about nine weeks before the board meeting. Do you have a plan?" asked Al.

"Pretty much. I started on it this morning. I just got in from a meeting with William Marks. He shared with me his process for sifting the wheat from the chaff, so to speak, and I'm going to start the search this afternoon," Bob replied.

"Martha has a friend she is going to push on you for the CFO position," Al warned.

"That's all I need, one of Martha's spies on my staff."

Bob's blood pressure was quickly rising.

"Thanks for the heads up Al. I will keep you informed on my progress."

"Bob, let me know if there is anything I can do," Al offered.

"Thanks Al."

Bob thought for a moment.

"Al, would you run interference with the board for me?"

"Sure. When you have your plan together, share it with me. It will help in my efforts. Good luck. I'd hate to have to replace our CEO."

And with that, Al hung up.

I'd hate to be replaced! Bob thought as he looked through the rest of the messages. They were all from board members. *I'll need to call them back this afternoon to keep a lid on this. Nothing like real pressure to change a lump of coal into a diamond.*

A knock at his door broke his train of thought. It was Diane Phillips.

"Where do you want to start, Boss?"

"I just spent the morning with William Marks." Bob paused for a few seconds. "And he shared with me his seven keys for hiring the right people. He briefly covered them last night, remember?"

Diane nodded.

"In addition to the technical competencies our new CFO needs that are already in the job description, we have identified eight key behavioral competencies. Here's the list," he said, sliding it over to Diane.

1. Leadership
2. Integrity
3. Trust and Respect
4. Develop Relationships
5. Team Building
6. Strategic Perspective
7. Concern for Quality
8. Collaboration

"William Marks is sending over the definitions and interview questions we selected this afternoon."

"Interesting," said Diane.

"This is what I want to do, before we begin our search." Bob thought for a moment. "Ask Ann to print out a copy of the job description and let's be sure it is up-to-date. I'll leave the sourcing to you. Can you to start sourcing candidates for the CFO today?"

"You bet!" responded Diane.

"Good. I'm going to call Martha Payton and schedule a meeting with the three of us for tomorrow. I want to review what I learned from William with the two of you, so we are all on the same page."

Bob really didn't want to do this but knew he should.

"I'll make time on my schedule," Diane replied. "Just let me know what time."

"You and I also need to do a competency analysis for the COO job. Let's do that tomorrow."

"Shouldn't we include Andrea and Teddy in the analysis? They both report to the COO and, as VP of Nursing and VP of Operations, they should be able to add value to the process."

"That's not a bad idea, Diane. See if they can join us. Any other suggestions?"

"Not now," she said, shaking her head.

"I'll let you know when Martha will be available. Let's get started."

Diane headed back to her office and Bob picked up the phone to call Martha.

CHAPTER 14

Setting the Stage

THE SOFT VOICE OF Martha's assistant answered the phone.

"Payton Accounting, how can I help you?"

"Good afternoon, Jan. This is Bob Paul. Is Martha available?"

"She's just finishing up a call, Mr. Paul. If you can hold for a moment, I'll slip a note in front of her and let her know you're on the line. Can you hold for a moment?"

"That's fine," Bob responded as Jan put him on hold and the elevator music started. Sure enough, Martha picked up a moment later.

"What's up Bob? By the way, I have a candidate for your CFO opening."

Bob still had to bite his tongue, but managed to sound authentic.

"Great, send me the résumé. By the way, Martha, thank you for your input this morning in analyzing the CFO position. I'm setting up a selection team, and since you're the CFO technical expert, I would like you to be part of the interview team."

Martha paused for a moment.

"Okay, Bob. What's your plan?"

"I want to schedule a prep meeting to share what I learned from William this morning, so each of the interview members will be on the same page. Can you free up about two hours tomorrow morning?"

"Who else do you have for the interview team?" Martha asked.

"I'm planning on Diane Phillips being the third team member. Are you game?" Bob pressed.

"Sure," Martha agreed, "how about . . . 10:30?"

"That will work. See you then. Oh . . . and you can bring your candidate's résumé with you."

Bob hung up while he still had his cool. *Boy, she can rub me wrong.*

He got up and went to the door.

"Ann, could you schedule a two-hour meeting starting at 10:30 tomorrow with Diane, Martha and myself? Then find out when Diane, Andrea, and Teddy can meet with me for about an hour."

"I'll take care of it. By the way, William Marks sent this envelope over."

Ann handed the large white envelope to Bob.

"Great!"

Bob was excited to see the analyzer and interview questions that William had promised.

CHAPTER 15

The Plan

BOB WAS FEELING THE stress of the situation as he walked into the hospital to start his day. Diane Phillips was already in the office and called his name as he walked by. Bob stuck his head in her door.

"Good morning Diane"

"Good morning Bob. I was wondering if you would consider interviewing Martin Miller for the CFO job."

"Martin Miller. Hmm . . . I'm not sure he's ready. Are you recommending him?"

"He approached me yesterday afternoon and expressed an interest, plus he has been number two under the last two CFOs. He does know our systems, culture, and objectives."

Diane paused, then looked Bob straight in the eyes.

"Yes, I would recommend we give him a shot."

"Okay, I wouldn't have thought of him as a candidate, but it would be a good test of this process." Bob was thinking out loud again.

"Are you ready for our meeting at 10:30 with Martha?"

"I'll be there and I have scheduled Andrea and Teddy to analyze the COO job at 3:30 this afternoon."

"Great. How is your sourcing going for COO candidates?"

"Actually," Diane began as she opened her file cabinet, "I have a résumé here from the COO at Memorial Hospital and I've been talking with Teddy. She doesn't feel ready yet, but she recommended a friend of hers over at General."

"Interesting. I want to move quickly and see if we can find some great talent. The nice thing about the process William Marks shared with me is that we will be able to assess the existing talent pool and see if there is a good candidate, *before* we start a big search."

"Would you like for me to put the word out anyway?" Diane asked.

"Hmm."

Bob thought for a moment. Things were moving quickly, but that was a good idea.

"Sure, it wouldn't hurt. Also, get with Ann and see if we can set up interviews with Teddy's friend and your candidate from Memorial Hospital for next week. I've got a meeting to deal with before our 10:30. See you in my office then."

Bob rushed off to his meeting, dropping off a few instructions with Ann, things to be handled for the 10:30 and 3:30 meetings.

At 10:30, Diane and Martha had gathered with Bob in his office. Bob turned to Martha.

"Martha, thank you for making time for me today. As I told you yesterday, I would like for you to participate in the selection of Community Hospital's new CFO."

Then, facing both, he went on.

"For the next couple of hours, I would first like to review what I learned from William Marks with the two of you, then strategize on how we will go about interviewing candidates."

"I will participate, if you include Pat Jackson, the candidate I recommend for the position," Martha demanded.

Bob had been afraid she would make such a demand, but had already given it some thought.

"I will include your candidate, as long as we agree to hold the candidate to the same standards we will hold the other candidates to."

Martha was quiet for a moment, then said, "Agreed."

Bob spent the next hour and a half bringing Diane and Martha up to speed. Then he shared with them the interview questions for the competencies that Martha and he had identified the previous day.

Now Bob wanted to get things rolling.

"Martha, I want to begin interviewing candidates as soon as possible. Diane has an internal candidate that I'm not sure is ready and you have your candidate. Can we schedule something for next week?"

"I have her résumé with me," said Martha, reaching for her briefcase.

"Great."

Bob smiled through clinched teeth, then put out his hand to take the résumé from Martha.

"Hmm, interesting. Some hospital experience. Okay. Diane, see if we can set up two interviews, one for Pat Jackson here and one for Martin Miller. We will start with these two and see how things shake out."

Bob covered each of the points William had covered with him the day before. Martha seemed to be on board, and that was a relief to Bob.

Time flew and it was soon time to do the analysis for the COO position with Andrea and Teddy. Martha left and Bob welcomed the two newcomers as they joined him and Diane.

Bob explained the process to Diane, Andrea, and Teddy, then proceeded with the analysis. It went quickly and forty-five minutes later, they had another set of competencies.

"Thank you for participating in this analysis. I think this will help a lot." Bob paused for a moment, then drew things to a close. "Andrea and Teddy, thank you again for your input. I'll let you get back to the more pressing things you have on your plates. Diane, could you give me a few more minutes?"

Andrea and Teddy headed out of the office as Bob asked Diane, "Have you set up the interviews for the COO yet?"

"Not yet. I wanted to wait until after we did the analysis."

"Good thought. Let's set up our interviews and get rolling."

CHAPTER 16

Pat Jackson's Interview

PAT JACKSON'S INTERVIEW WAS scheduled first. Martha, Diane, and Bob met in his office prior to the meeting and Bob assigned specific questions for each of them to ask.

Ann stuck her head in the office door.

"Bob, Pat Jackson is in the lobby. Do you want me to go get her?"

"No, thank you, Ann. This is important. I'll go greet her and bring her back myself."

Bob rose and excused himself.

Five minutes later, everyone was seated around the small, round conference table. Bob introduced Pat Jackson, a slender and attractive woman who appeared to be middle-aged.

Bob handled the introductions, then began.

"Pat, I want to set the stage for today's interview. We have done an analysis of the CFO position you are interviewing for and have identified a number of competencies essential for success. Those have been the basis from which we have created interview questions to help us gain insight into your potential fit for the position."

Bob paused and Diane jumped in.

"The nice thing about these questions is that you already know all of the answers, because we will be talking about your experiences. We will want you to take a few moments to think of an example from your experiences to share with us for each question we ask."

Martha followed.

"As a help to you, when you think of an example, tell us where and when the example took place, the name of someone involved, the challenge you faced, the action you took, and the results you got."

Bob was not only pleased that this was a team interview, but that his team had embraced the concepts behind the process.

"Do you have any questions?" Bob asked.

Pat shook her head. She seemed calm, confident, and ready to get started.

"Okay, let's jump right in then. Leadership, it has been said, means getting people to do things because they want to. When have you been successful in stimulating others to take personal responsibility? How did you do it?"

Pat thought about it for a few moments, than her eyes lit up.

"Yes, in my current position at Barnes Manufacturing, my boss...."

"Who is . . .?" Bob asked.

"Oh, I'm sorry, Peter Stans is the CEO. Anyway, Peter dropped an expansion project with a short fuse in my lap. The first thing I did was pull my team together and we strategized how we could pull it off. We broke the work up into packages and, for developmental purposes, I gave my team members the choice of which packages they would take responsibility for, in addition to their regular jobs.

This approach really worked well. We kept up on our regular work and beat our deadline by a week."

"Thank you, Pat, for that example," said Diane. "Now if you would, think of a time when you weren't proud of your ability to get people to take personal responsibility, and what you learned from it."

Pat thought for a moment, then said, "Yeah, I had an Accounts Receivable supervisor, Tony McCord, who worked for me not long after I joined Barnes Manufacturing. I think he wanted my job. I told him that I'd help develop him for his next career step.

"Anyway, I couldn't take the time to deal with him. Over a period of a month, I didn't feel I could get him turned around and fired him. What I learned was not to promise to help someone if I really planned on firing them anyway."

It was Martha's turn.

"I have the next question. Some rules seem to be made to be broken. Share with me an example of when you did what was right, even when no one was watching."

"This one is easy," said Pat. "My first boss, Jack Ryan, taught me that when leaders ask what two plus two is, accountants should not respond with, 'Four.' Rather, they should ask, 'What do you want it to be?' Which leads me to my example.

"Last summer Peter Stans, my current boss, came to me and asked me to discretely write off some loans that were made to himself and the COO. It took some creativity, but I pulled it off and it wasn't even noticed by our accounting firm. Sometimes it takes bending the rules to accomplish objectives."

The interview continued through the rest of the sixteen structured interview questions.

"Pat, we've asked you a lot of questions," said Bob. "You have provided us with a great deal of information to analyze. Is there anything we didn't ask that we should have?"

Pat thought for a moment and said, "No, I can't think of anything."

"Do you have any questions of us?" asked Diane.

Pat had come armed with a fistful of questions about Community Hospital and the next ten minutes were spent covering them.

After Bob had walked Pat out the lobby and thanked her for making time for the interview, he went back to his office to rate the interview. He found Martha and Pat reviewing their interview notes.

Bob started by explaining that he would read the competency definition and ask for one of the four ratings: strong evidence candidate lacks the competency; some evidence candidate lacks the competency; some evidence candidate has the competency, or; strong evidence candidate has the competency.

"The rating should be based on the quality, fit and verifiability of the responses," Bob explained.

Bob read the first competency definition.

"Leadership: Able to develop and inspire others to take personal responsibility; get factions with competing perspectives to learn from one another; integrate efforts and talents of team members; lead people past status quo to achieve new levels of excellence."

Diane started. "I would rate her as showing some evidence she has the competency. She gave a great example of how she pulled off the project with her team. And that covers the first component of the definition: Able to develop and inspire others to take personal responsibility.

"When I asked about a time when she blew it, her example of failure was plausible and I wanted to get a balanced picture of her skills. I wouldn't hold her response against her."

Martha jumped in. "I actually agree with that assessment."

Bob nodded his head and put a check mark in the rating box. Then he read the next definition.

"Integrity: Able to demonstrate sound ethical behaviors; show consistency between words and actions; do what is right even when no one is watching; consistently comply with organizational values."

Martha didn't waste any time giving her rating.

"Pat and I went to school together and I thought I knew her well, but her response here scared me to death. It really disappointed me. Plus, she lacked consistency between words and actions in her response to Diane's leadership follow-up question. Remember when she said she had learned that she shouldn't make a promise she wasn't willing to keep and then fired Tony McCord? I'd rate this one as strong evidence candidate lacks the competency."

Bob and Diane agreed and he made another check mark.

The ratings continued through each of the competencies. After about ten minutes they finished their ratings.

Bob looked at the rating form, then at Martha.

"Martha? How do you feel about Pat's fit for the CFO job?"

Looking solemn and shaking her head, Martha said, "Not good, not good at all."

Candidate Rating Form

Position Title: <u>Chief Financial Officer</u>   Candidate: <u>Pat Jackson</u>

Interviewer: <u>Bob Paul, Martha Payton</u>   Date: _____
Diane Phillips

Rating Anchors	Strong Evidence Candidate Lacks Competency	Some Evidence Candidate Lacks Competency	Some Evidence Candidate Has Competency	Strong Evidence Candidate Has Competency
Behavioral Competencies				
1. Leadership			✓	
2. Integrity	✓			
3. Trust and Respect		✓		
4. Develop Relationships			✓	
5. Team Building				✓
6. Strategic Perspective			✓	
7. Concern for Quality			✓	
8. Collaboration				✓
Technical Competencies				
1. Manage Accounting Function			✓	
2. Financial Strategies And Plans			✓	
3. Financial Modeling				✓
4. Budget Reporting				✓
5. Budget Decisions			✓	
6. Secure Capital				✓

Recommended for Position: [   ] Yes   [✓] No

CHAPTER 17

Martin Miller's Interview

AS THE TEAM FINISHED rating Pat's interview, Bob sat back, satisfied with the team's collaboration. The process seemed to be working well. There were concerns about Pat, as a candidate, but Bob was happy the team was able to identify them through the structured interview process. He was ready for the next candidate, Martin Miller.

Martin was a stocky African American man in his late forties. A quiet man, he had been with Community Hospital for over nine years.

Bob was a bit startled to find Martin already at Ann's desk when he opened the interview room door.

"Martin, please come in," he said.

Martin recognized Diane, who greeting him warmly, and Bob introduced Martha. Martin seemed a bit nervous.

"Are you ready?" Bob asked.

Martin nodded and said, "Thank you for giving me a chance."

"Before we begin the interview, I want you to know how we are going to go about the interview," Bob said, beginning the explanation.

Martha and Diane chimed in, the three interviewers setting the stage for Martin as they had done for Pat Jackson.

Then Bob began with the first questions.

"Martin, it has been said that leadership means getting people to do things because they want to. When have you been successful in stimulating others to take personal responsibility? How did you do it?"

Martin's pause was longer than Pat's, so Bob broke the tension at about ten seconds.

"Take your time."

Then Martin slowly began.

"About two years ago, I was acting CFO, while we were looking for a replacement. The former CFO had been kind of a recluse and Mr. Peters, who was the CEO, asked me to try and pull things back together again.

"The first thing I did was to meet with each member of the staff, review their responsibilities, and set some specific goals with each person to be accomplished in the next thirty days. There were a few individuals who had competing personal agendas and I had to get them together to iron out their differences, which helped them learn from one another. I also spent some time understanding what motivated each person and tried to use the unique talents of each team member.

"Well, the result surprised even Mr. Peters. Each member of the team stepped up, took personal responsibility for their goals, and even exceeded them.

"I continued to recognize and help each of them to achieve a new level of excellence, even after the new CFO took over."

This time Martha followed up.

"Martin, think of a time when you weren't proud of your ability to get people to take personal responsibility. Tell us what happened."

This one was easier for Martin. "Before I came to Community, I was at General Hospital. This must have been almost ten years ago. I worked for a really good boss, June Werner, and she had given me an opportunity to lead a project team of twelve individuals from various parts of the hospital. Almost everyone was easy to work with, except one individual who didn't want to be on the team and wouldn't come to the meetings or take any assignments. I met privately with him and tried to get him to be a contributor. His response was, 'Look I didn't want to be made part of this team, but my boss insisted.' So I decided to pick up his responsibilities in order to meet our goal."

He paused. Then, after a moment, continued.

"You know, after the project was a success, he wanted credit. At least I had kept June informed on what was happening and she let his boss know that he shouldn't get any credit."

He paused again.

"You know, I wasn't really proud of my ability at that point."

Diane had the next question.

"Martin, some rules seem to be made to be broken. Share with me an example of when you did what was right even when no one was watching."

Martin was getting the hang of the questions and only had to think for a brief moment before answering.

"Last year, I was working with the CPA from Accent Accounting who was auditing for our annual financial report. I was working late one night, after everyone had gone home, and noticed that there was a significant reporting error in our 401(k) contributions. What I did was document the error and make the corrections. Then I brought it to the attention of the CPA. The nice thing was that the CPA had noticed that the numbers seemed odd the day before, but had not gotten into it yet. She went to Mr. Peters and said my actions to correct, document, and bring the problem to her attention showed a great deal of integrity for the hospital."

The interview continued until the team had asked all sixteen of the structured interview questions.

Bob asked Diane and Martha if they had any additional questions for Martin and they shook their heads. Wrapping up the interview as he had done with Pat, Bob asked Martin if he had any questions for them and they spent a few minutes with his questions.

Bob explained to Martin that they needed to rate his responses against the competency definitions and would let him know how he did the following day.

Martin again thanked them for the opportunity to interview for the position, excused himself, and left.

"Diane, did you prep him for the interview?" Martha asked.

"No . . . things have been moving way too fast. Except for setting up the interview, I haven't spoken to him. Why?"

"He surprised me with his professionalism," Martha replied. "He really surprised me. I hadn't seen him in this light before."

"Let's rate his responses," Bob suggested. "Shall we start at the beginning with the leadership category?"

"Starting at the beginning is always good," teased Martha.

Bob smiled.

"Okay, here's the definition for Leadership: Able to develop and inspire others to take personal responsibility; get factions with competing perspectives to learn from one another; integrate efforts and talents of team members; lead people past status quo to achieve new levels of excellence."

"Martin's leadership examples were really strong," began Martha. "He showed real leadership. He got his team members to take personal responsibility, got individuals with competing perspectives to learn from one another and effectively use their various talents, and went above and beyond in helping them achieve excellence. I'd rate him as providing strong evidence he has the competency."

"Wow," Diane nodded, "I'd have to agree. You covered it very well."

Bob asked, "Were you here when that acting CFO example took place, Diane?"

"Yes, I had forgotten about that situation, but that is how it happened."

"Okay, strong evidence the candidate has the competency?" Bob asked.

Both Martha and Diane agreed.

The team then went through the entire rating process. It was becoming easier. Diane, Martha, and Bob found that Martin was a really strong candidate.

"Martha, we have rated Martin with mostly strong evidence of having each of the competencies necessary for success. What are your thoughts?" Bob asked.

"We could keep the door open and look around to see who else might be out there, but you would be hard pressed to find someone stronger than Martin. Plus, he knows Community Hospital," Martha counseled.

Diane added, "He is also well respected by the rest of the staff. His learning curve would be very short."

Bob thought for a few moments, then nodded his head.

"I hate to admit it, but my initial bias was that he wasn't ready. His examples of past actions were very good, though. He's changed my mind.

"Thank you both for helping me with this process. Martin Miller it is. Diane, would you prepare an offer?"

"You bet, Boss," said Diane.

"That's one position filled with a great candidate," Martha admitted, "but you still have another key position you need to get back on track, and less than eight weeks before the board meeting."

"You're not going to let up, are you, Martha?" Bob replied, trying to sound pleasant.

"Nope," Martha called out, over her shoulder, as she left.

Candidate Rating Form

Position Title: Chief Financial Officer Candidate: Martin Miller

Interviewer: Bob Paul, Martha Payton Date:
Diane Phillips

Rating Anchors	Strong Evidence Candidate Lacks Competency	Some Evidence Candidate Lacks Competency	Some Evidence Candidate Has Competency	Strong Evidence Candidate Has Competency
Behavioral Competencies				
1. Leadership				✓
2. Integrity				✓
3. Trust and Respect				✓
4. Develop Relationships				✓
5. Team Building				✓
6. Strategic Perspective			✓	
7. Concern for Quality				✓
8. Collaboration				✓
Technical Competencies				
1. Manage Accounting Function				✓
2. Financial Strategies And Plans				✓
3. Financial Modeling				✓
4. Budget Reporting				✓
5. Budget Decisions				✓
6. Secure Capital			✓	

Recommended for Position: [✓] Yes   [   ] No

CHAPTER 18

The COO Interview Team

THINGS WERE MOVING UNUSUALLY fast, but Bob needed to keep things on track. His next move was to get an interview team together for the COO position. He had an idea and picked up the phone to call William.

"Hello," William answered in the strong and confident voice that Bob knew well.

"William, this is Bob Paul. Thank you again for your interview coaching. I'm one step closer to having my team together again."

"Glad to hear it," said William, sounding pleased. "Did you include Martha?"

"Yes, and that worked out better than I could have hoped. Plus, Diane Phillips is up to speed as well and was the third member of the interview team."

"So what is your next step?" William asked.

"My next step is to interview two potential candidates for the COO position and I was wondering if you would be willing to join Diane and me on this interview team?" Bob asked.

"Hmm, when do you plan on getting started?"

"In the next couple of days, depending on your availability. We have two potential candidates to consider before we broaden the search."

"Okay, I can make time. Who are you considering?"

"A guy from Memorial named Mike VanBell. And do you remember Teddy Barr?" Bob asked. "She recommended Judith Bass from General Hospital."

"I do remember Teddy," William replied, "but Mike VanBell and Judith Bass are new names to me."

Bob wanted to keep things moving.

"William, do you have your calendar handy? Today is Monday. How about either Thursday afternoon or Friday morning?"

"Both work for me," William responded.

"I'll see if I can get them scheduled," Bob replied, excited to get things moving. "Thanks, William. I really appreciate your support."

CHAPTER 19

Judith Bass's Interview

JUDITH BASS WAS SCHEDULED for a Thursday afternoon interview. William, Diane, and Bob met a bit early in Bob's office. They gathered around the small round conference table and divided up the questions.

Ann stuck her head into Bob's office.

"Judith is here for her interview. Do you want to greet her personally?"

"Yes, thank you, Ann."

Bob rose and excused himself.

Five minutes later, everyone was seated around the conference table and Bob had made the introductions.

Judith Bass was a slender, tall woman with silver hair. She seemed eager to get started.

Bob began by welcoming Judith to the interview and explaining how the interview was structured.

Judith smiled uneasily.

"Judith," Bob began, "I want to set the stage for today's interview."

He then explained the process, just as he had done for the CFO candidates. Diane jumped in to let Judith know that Judith's answers would be drawn from her experience. William added the last piece, letting her know they wanted the name of someone involved when she gave an example, along with the challenge, the action taken, and the results achieved.

"Okay, let's get started. Leadership, it has been said, means getting people to do things because they want to. When have you been successful in stimulating others to take personal responsibility? How did you do it?"

"That's an interesting question. Let me think for a moment," Judith said. "I'm not sure what you are looking for, but two years ago, when I was tapped to be the COO at General Hospital, I spent a lot of time talking with people all around the hospital during my first few weeks. One of the common complaints was that things had become very bureaucratic with lots of red tape. Some people liked the restrictions, but most caregivers felt their hands were tied and that they couldn't give truly good patient service."

Bob cut in.

"Judith, could you give me the name of your CEO?"

Judith paused, then said, "Yes, his name is Brian Horne."

"Thanks, Judith. Please continue with your story."

"Okay, let's see . . . oh yes, I also spent time looking at what few metrics we had. The patient satisfaction numbers were in the mid-forties. As I reviewed them with my staff, they shrugged. Margaret Peters, my VP of Support Services, even said, 'What do you expect with all of the restrictions we have?'

"Well, most of my staff felt it was hopeless, but they were willing to try. The first thing I did was to challenge them to take personal responsibility to identify problem policies and procedures and make recommendations to modify them so we could really be of service. And I promised to spend time on each shift talking with employees who had suggestions.

"I also started a weekly thirty-minute personal action discussion with each of my direct reports. Well, things started to move slowly, until one nurse, Kathy Kroop, stuck her neck out and suggested that the policy of only allowing the charge nurse to talk to doctors was a time waster.

"So I talked with my staff and they agreed. I made the change immediately and ran it by the Chief Medical Officer, Ken Drake. Then I started a communication process with the Docs that has really enhanced productivity and the nurses' feelings of self-worth.

"With a number of changes like that, we have been able to improve our patient satisfaction numbers by twenty-eight points. My nurses are taking more personal responsibility in meeting patient needs."

"Thank you Judith."

William took the lead on the next question, "If you will, describe a situation in which you built a relationship by demonstrating awareness of someone's needs. What was the situation and what did you do?"

Judith thought for a quick moment and then began. "About six or eight months ago my VP of Nursing . . ."

"Who was?" Diane softly asked.

"Oh, yes. Sorry. I forgot. Her name is Kristen Laidlaw. Anyway,

Kristen came to me because she was having trouble working with one of her nurse managers, Debi Diaz. I asked her when and where she was scheduled to work, made a note and scheduled some time to meet with her.

"Debi was scheduled the next day in the emergency room, and things seemed quiet enough, so I asked her to take a few minutes to talk with me. I explained that Kristen had come to me and she was concerned.

"She asked, 'In what way?'

"Well, I continued in as kind a way as I could, saying that Kristen had told me she'd had a one-on-one with Debi in which she'd raised a number of issues: that Debi showed little to no empathy with regard to the impact of her actions on others; that Debi's nurses felt they had better not cross her or disagree with her, even if she was wrong, and; that nurses were bailing out of her unit faster than they could be replaced.

"Well, she just broke down crying. Finally she pulled herself together and we talked about it. She had been a great nurse and was tapped to be a manager and thrown into the position.

"I asked her if she wanted to be a great manager or just go back to being a nurse. She decided she wanted to become a great manager, but needed help. Together we outlined a plan for her to be mentored by Kristen and myself, then we set some goals with clear expectations.

"It is interesting to me that the time I have spent mentoring Debi—and coaching Kristen in her efforts to mentor Debi—have built some very strong relationships between the three of us. Debi has made some great changes in her leadership style and turnover in her department has gone down to near zero. I'm really proud of her."

Bob, William, and Diane continued through each of the sixteen questions for the COO. Once they had finished the interview, Bob began to wrap up the interview.

"Judith, we have asked you a lot of questions and you have provided us with a lot of information to analyze. Is there anything we didn't ask that we should have?"

Judith shook her head.

"No, I can't think of anything. This has been the most thorough interview I have ever had."

Diane then asked if Judith had any questions for them. Judith flipped the notebook she had in front of her to a page with questions. She asked several questions about the hospital and the position.

When Judith's last question was answered, Bob explained that the interview team needed to rate her responses against the competency definitions and would let her know how she did in the next couple of days.

Judith gave a nervous smile, stood, and shook everyone's hands. Bob walked with her to the lobby.

"Bob, I wasn't really thinking of changing jobs, but you seem to be serious about finding your next COO. If you decide to select me, I'd like to join your team."

Candidate Rating Form

Position Title: Chief Financial Officer   Candidate: Judith Bass

Interviewer: Bob Paul, Diane Phillips   Date: _____
William Marks

Rating Anchors	Strong Evidence Candidate Lacks Competency	Some Evidence Candidate Lacks Competency	Some Evidence Candidate Has Competency	Strong Evidence Candidate Has Competency
Behavioral Competencies				
1. Leadership				✓
2. Integrity				✓
3. Trust and Respect				✓
4. Develop Relationships				✓
5. Team Building				✓
6. Strategic Perspective			✓	
7. Concern for Quality				✓
8. Collaboration				✓
Technical Competencies				
1. Hospital Strategic Direction			✓	
2. Hospital Accreditation				✓
3. Achieve Business Targets				✓
4. Service Quality Improvement				✓
5. Budget Decisions			✓	
6. Facility Planning				✓

Recommended for Position: [✓] Yes   [   ] No

CHAPTER 20

Mike VanBell's Interview

FRIDAY MORNING WAS BRIGHT, cool, and crisp. William and Diane met Bob in his office to prepare for Mike VanBell's interview. Bob was eager to continue with the interview process, feeling more and more confident about his team's ability to make good selections from among the candidates.

Once again, he thanked William, confiding how grateful he was for an interview process that really zeroed in on what he needed to know about the candidates. He felt certain he was on his way to building a great executive team.

Ann stuck her head into Bob's office.

"Mike is in the lobby for his interview. Are you ready to get him?"

"You bet," said Bob.

He quickly returned with Mike, who was a bit taller than him, had jet black hair, and sported a big smile. Bob introduced him to William and Diane as Ann brought Mike a glass of water.

"Before we begin the interview, I want you to know how we are going to go about it."

Bob, William and Diane set the stage, just as they had done for Judith Bass.

"Any questions?" asked Bob.

"No, it sounds straightforward to me," Mike replied.

"Great. Let's get started, then. Leadership, it has been said, means getting people to do things because they want to. When have you been successful in stimulating others to take personal responsibility? How did you do it?"

"I do that all of the time," Mike said with confidence. "It seems that no one wants to take personal responsibility to do anything. What I would do to motivate people is get them to focus."

"Mike, I'm glad you do it all the time," interjected William. His deep voice was soft and encouraging, but also firm. "This should be easy then. I want you to think of a specific time in the last six months when you used your leadership skills to get someone to take personal responsibility for a job they probably hadn't wanted to do.

"I want you to tell me when and where it took place, who was involved, the challenge you faced, the action you took, and the result you got."

Mike looked at William with glazed-over eyes, as if he were a deer in the headlights. He stared in silence for what seemed a long time but was, in reality, only about seven seconds. Then looking away for a moment, he began his answer.

"Okay, here's an example . . . no that's not a good one."

There was silence for another ten seconds.

"Take your time, Mike," Bob said.

Mike smiled uneasily, his confidence gone.

"Okay, I had a nursing director at Memorial Hospital about a year ago. I inherited her and she was a piece of work."

"What was her name?" Bob probed.

"Elizabeth Burke. Anyway, not only would she not take personal responsibility for the way things were running, she wouldn't hold others accountable either." Mike appeared to be regaining his confidence as he spoke. "So, I scheduled a meeting with her to put my cards on the table and told her what I expected. Elizabeth was very defensive, but I won her over when I explained that I was going to hold her accountable and she would need to hold her nurses accountable, or she could get a new job."

Mike paused for a moment, as if for effect, then went on.

"Anyway, things got better fast. Her nurses were not too happy with the changes I made, but Elizabeth implemented them very well."

Diane asked a follow-up question.

"Mike, how is Elizabeth doing now?"

Mike hesitated, as if he didn't want to share that information.

"She left about two months later."

"Mike," Bob said, "if you would, think of a time when you felt you used your leadership skills and someone really got excited about an assignment they were responsible for completing."

He was seeking a contrary example to balance the previous one.

Mike seemed stumped again. Then, after a moment, he began.

"Last week, my assistant, Rose Bloom, wanted to take the lead on a fund-raiser, to buy materials to make quilts for kids with cancer. I told her it was a waste of time and made a joke about it, but gave her the okay. Anyway, she was able to raise over $5,000. I understand that the Women's Guild will be able to make over a hundred quilts in the next two years."

Diane asked the next question.

"Mike, if you will, describe a situation in which you built a relationship by demonstrating awareness of someone's needs. What was the situation and what did you do?"

"That's an easy one," Mike replied. "Last month I had a Doc—"

"Who was . . .?" William prompted.

"Oh, yeah. Doctor Clarence Greene. Anyway, he came to me and requested that we get a portable CT scanner for the intensive care unit. I had been told that Doctor Greene had derailed the previous COO, so I played it cagey. I had already been investigating the possibility of getting a CT scanner. In fact, I had already picked a supplier and had the contract on my desk. I decided not to tell him about my plan and to let him think it was his idea.

"That decision bought me a lot of points with Doctor Greene and the medical staff when I rolled the new unit in. I felt really good about pulling one over on them."

William, Diane, and Bob continued through each of the sixteen questions for the COO. Once they had finished, Bob began to wrap up the interview.

"Mike, we have asked you a lot of questions and you have provided us with a lot of information to analyze. Is there anything that we didn't ask that we should have?"

Mike was quick with, "Yes, Community Hospital has a great reputation and I would like to be part of the team."

"We appreciate your enthusiasm, Mike," said Bob. "Do you have any questions of us before we finish?"

Mike had come prepared with a couple of questions and the interview team answered them. Then, as with the earlier candidates, Bob explained that the team needed to rate his responses against the competency definitions and would let him know how he did in the next couple of days.

Mike smiled and he and Bob walked together back out to the lobby.

"Bob, that was a very thorough interview. How do you think I did?"

"Really, I don't know. As thorough as we were, we need to be just as thorough in how we rate your responses against the competencies. Thanks again for spending time with us today."

He shook Mike's hand and waved good-by as he headed back to his office.

William and Diane were already reviewing their notes on the first competency.

"Where are we?" Bob asked.

"We just read the definition for Leadership," Diane responded. "I'll do it again. Leadership: Able to develop and inspire others to take personal responsibility; get factions with competing perspectives to learn from one another; integrate efforts and talents of team members; lead people past status quo to achieve new levels of excellence."

"Okay, I'll start" said William. "As I reread his examples, my feeling is that his leadership style would not be a good fit for Community, not because he held Elizabeth accountable, but for the way he went about it."

"That is an interesting assessment, William. I didn't get the feeling that he really engaged those who worked for him when he described how he felt he was a leader by allowing his assistant to do the fundraiser," Diane added.

"So, would we agree there is strong evidence that Mike lacks the kind of leadership competency that Community Hospital needs?" Bob asked.

Both William and Diane agreed.

"Let's talk about the 'Develop Relationships' competency next," Bob suggested. "I'll read it this time. Develop Relationships: Able to build credibility and rapport with others; initiate the building of a cooperative relationship with others; demonstrate awareness of others' needs; use appropriate humor to ease tension, without putting others down."

"His example here seemed weak to me," said William. "Do you remember his example of purchasing equipment for Doctor Greene?"

Bob and Diane nodded and William continued.

"He did build credibility and rapport with Doctor Greene, though I'm not sure how he initiated building a cooperative relationship beyond that. And he went about it in a way that lacked integrity. He actually seemed to enjoy putting one over on the doctors. Also, remember how he handled the situation with Elizabeth and his assistant? Condescending and belittling? I would have to rate him as 'Some Evidence Candidate Lacks Competency.'"

Bob and Diane agreed. They continued to review Mike's rating form and completed the rest of the competency ratings.

Candidate Rating Form

Position Title: <u>Chief Financial Officer</u>   Candidate: <u>Mike VanBell</u>

Interviewer: <u>Bob Paul, Diane Phillips</u>   Date: _____
<u>William Marks</u>

Rating Anchors	Strong Evidence Candidate Lacks Competency	Some Evidence Candidate Lacks Competency	Some Evidence Candidate Has Competency	Strong Evidence Candidate Has Competency
Behavioral Competencies				
1. Leadership	✓			
2. Integrity		✓		
3. Trust and Respect			✓	
4. Develop Relationships		✓		
5. Team Building			✓	
6. Strategic Perspective				✓
7. Concern for Quality				✓
8. Collaboration		✓		
Technical Competencies				
1. Hospital Strategic Direction		✓		
2. Hospital Accreditation				✓
3. Achieve Business Targets			✓	
4. Service Quality Improvement			✓	
5. Budget Decisions			✓	
6. Facility Planning		✓		

Recommended for Position: [   ] Yes   [✓] No

CHAPTER 21

The New Team

"BOB, I REALIZE THAT we are comparing just two candidates here. But one nice thing about using this process is that when you find a really qualified candidate who has the right competencies and would be a great fit with Community Hospital's culture, you don't need to spend a lot of additional time looking," said William. He paused for a moment, and then continued. "I suggest that you seriously consider Judith as your next COO. She would be a good fit for your team."

"I like her as well, but you don't you think I need to see if there is anyone else out there we should consider?" Diane asked.

"You can if you want to," William responded. "Think of it this way Diane: In traditional selection processes interviewers parade a number of candidates and pick the best they find. Not knowing if they would be successful, they are just the best of the group, and maybe none are qualified.

"Here we have established a set of selection criteria and found a candidate who is strong in almost every competency."

"I think you are right William," Bob chimed in. "I trust the process and what we learned from each candidate. Judith would be a good fit here at Community Hospital."

"Diane, are you good with this decision?" Bob asked.

"Yes, I agree. Should I make up an offer for Judith?"

"Make it so," Bob responded, and they all laughed.

"Thank you for all of your help, William. I have really learned a lot. Funny how the process helped me avoid a candidate Martha put forward and led me to a candidate I thought was weaker on paper than the one I thought I wanted," Bob confided. "But I'm pleased with the outcome. This will be a great team.

"Something else is bothering me though. One of the concerns I have had is whether we have the right people at the bedside, serving our patients. Can this process be used at all levels of the organization?"

"Why not?" both William and Diane responded.

"Then, Diane, let's start making that happen as well. Thanks again, William. I owe you one."

Everyone rose and wandered out of Bob's office. Diane went to her office to prepare the offer letter and William shook Bob's hand and walked confidently down the hall toward the lobby door.

Bob thought for a moment. *Now is the time for action.* He headed for Martin's office. Not only did he want to fill in his new CFO about the decision he'd just made, he also wanted to move things forward.

"Martin, do you have a moment?"

"Sure, Bob, what is it?"

"I wanted to let you know that we have selected a new COO, Judith Bass. I also wanted to chat about what you plan on doing with your department and in moving the new addition forward."

"Good news about the COO choice," said Martin. Then he went on to lay out his plans.

Bob approved.

"I sure feel a sense of relief having gone through this learning process and the outcomes," Bob confided.

"I can understand the feeling. I really appreciate your giving me the chance," Martin replied.

"You earned it, Martin."

Bob left Martin's office and returned to his own. His mind was rushing through all of the challenges that needed to be addressed in the five weeks before the board meeting.

"Ann, as soon as Judith Bass has accepted her offer, would you set up a lunch or dinner meeting with her? I would like to get her started thinking about how we might get back on track."

"I'll get right on it," said Ann, already reaching for the phone.

"Thanks Ann."

Bob knew he had a lot to do before he was out of the woods, but felt a sense of hope for the first time in a long time.

CHAPTER 22

The Board Meeting

THE SUN WAS BRIGHT and there was a nice crispness in the air. It was a board meeting Wednesday and Bob Paul was feeling good about the upcoming meeting.

With two hours before the start of the meeting, Bob headed for Martin's office to be sure everything was ready.

"Good morning Martin. Do we have everything ready for the board meeting?"

"Yes, sir," responded Martin with confidence.

"Great! I want you to present the financials to the board. It will be a great way for you to develop credibility with them. I need to touch base with Diane and Judith. See you at 10:00."

Bob rushed off to Judith's office.

Judith wasn't in her office, so Bob went to Diane's office, where he found Judith and Diane in serious discussion.

"What's up?"

"Bob, Diane and I were just discussing a rumor I heard last night that a couple of board members were still unhappy with you and may move to have you replaced," Judith said, looking a bit worried.

"I thought I had that under control. Well, there is nothing we can do about that now. Is everything else ready for the meeting?"

Both Judith and Diane nodded their heads.

Bob went to his office.

"Ann, ask the front desk to let me know when the board members start arriving."

"Will do," Ann replied and reached for the phone.

After reviewing his notes and presentation one more time, Bob gazed out the window and tried to decide how to deal with this latest challenge.

Ann stuck her head into Bob's office, and said, "Bob, the board members are arriving. Do you want to be in the boardroom as they arrive?"

"You bet. And let Martin, Judith and Diane know as well."

Bob was anxious to put forth a positive front as he headed toward the boardroom. He arrived just as Albert Carlson, the Chairman of the Board, did.

"Good morning Al. How are you this morning?"

"I'm doing well this morning, Bob. Are you ready?"

"You bet. I feel good about how things are going," Bob said with confidence as they walked into the board room.

In the next five minutes, the board room filled and Albert called the meeting to order. After reviewing and approving the last meeting's minutes, Albert turned the meeting over to Bob.

"Since our last Board meeting, we have selected a new CFO, Martin Miller. I want to introduce him to you and let you know that he has hit the ground running. I also want to recognize his efforts in turning around our revenue cycle. I will let him fill in the details, but I am happy to announce that revenues are up 22%. Martin."

"Let me first point out that I got help from some consultants who specialize in turning around revenue cycles. We began by looking at our admissions process—our first encounter with the patient—then went on to devise more effective coding processes and quicker billing."

Martin methodically described his effort.

"Martin, why did you use an outside consultant?" a board member asked.

"We wanted a fresh look at our existing systems and processes. We've been doing it the same way for years and I thought we could do it better."

"Good thinking. Thank you, Martin," said Albert with an almost imperceptible sly smile.

The other board members nodded their heads in approval.

"Bob, I think you made a very good selection decision with Martin," Albert added.

"I agree, Albert," said Bob. "Martin has made a number of insightful improvements in the last month. His plans to make additional changes have the staff excited. He has outlined them and their potential benefits in our report. He has also done a great job building the moral in his department."

Bob waited a few moments for the board members to scan the report.

"Any questions?"

Bob looked around the table. Every board member seemed satisfied.

"If we could, I would like to move on. Also since our last Board meeting, we have had Judith Bass join us as the new COO. She brings a lot of experience to us, both as a nurse and as an operations leader. Please welcome Judith Bass to our team."

The board gave tentative, polite approval.

Judith stood and stepped away from the table, then moved to the front of the boardroom to make her presentation. She was thorough and professional, impressing almost everyone in the room. Her plans for controlling both the costs and the schedule of the new addition were met with nods of approval.

She finished her presentation with, "This community is important to me. It is my home and I want to help make it a better place to live. I hope to get to know each of you over the coming months as we work to improve patient and employee satisfaction, as well as get this addition completed."

Again Albert was complimentary about Bob's selection decision.

Kim Moss, one of Martha Payton's allies, bluntly broke into the exchange.

"Albert, I want to ask the other board members if they are satisfied with Bob Paul's efforts over the last year."

Martha was first to respond.

"Before I give my two cents, I'd like to hear what Bob has learned and done in the last couple of months to overcome the leadership problems this hospital has faced."

All eyes shot to Bob.

"That is a good question, Martha. I will admit that I made a couple of bad hiring decisions when I first became CEO. Since then, I have learned a lot about how to make informed hiring decisions. You might say I learned that interviewing is a process, not an event."

"Bob, would you share an outline of what you learned?" Martha asked.

"Sure. Among the things that have kept me awake at night are several nagging questions. Do we have the right people? The right people in leadership positions? The right people taking care of patients? William Marks taught me that there are seven keys to selecting extraordinary leaders.

"First, it is critical—the absolute foundation—to clearly define the position requirements for any job *before* you start your search. Essentially, you cannot effectively tell if a candidate is qualified for a job if you don't establish criteria in advance.

"Second, I needed to create a structured job-related interview from the position requirements. After all, if I'm going to compare apples to apples, I need a consistent set of data to work from."

He paused.

"Third, I learned that past *actions* are the best predictors of future actions and I learned how to use past-event interview questions to get at those past actions.

"You know," Bob thought out loud, "I think I'll call this Action Interviewing."

He continued.

"Forth, I learned that I should not go it alone when making selection decisions. Hence, I used a team approach with three people on each interview. In fact, Martha Payton was a member of the selection team for the CFO."

Some board members, including Kim Moss, looked shocked.

Bob continued, seeming to ignore the shocked looks, but feeling a bit of satisfaction.

"Fifth—and this was a hard one—I needed to learn to control my biases and first impressions. Kind of reminds me of the *Dragnet* line, 'Just the facts, ma'am.'

"Sixth, I learned how important it was to establish rating guides in advance. I have always gone by the seat of my pants because I felt I would know a great candidate when I saw him or her. Well, I was wrong. Having a set of rating guidelines really helped.

"Seventh—last but not least—I learned how to rate candidates by consensus. Since I had a team helping me interview each candidate, having their input on the rating was important."

"Okay Bob, one more question. What are you going to do to keep this new team focused and engaged?" Martha asked.

This question blindsided Bob.

"I'm not sure I understand what you mean?"

"Bob, you need to think that through and have a plan for us at our next board meeting. But for now," Martha turned to Albert, addressing this last comment to him, "I think Bob has things going in the right direction."

Martha sat back in her chair and looked at Bob. "That is your leadership challenge: building an engaged and innovative environment."

"So we don't want to push for Bob's removal?" Kim whispered to Martha.

"Not now. He may be able to pull this together after all," Martha whispered back.

"With that, I move that we adjourn this meeting," announced Albert.

"I second that motion," said Martha.

"All in favor?"

Albert smiled as he got a chorus of "Aye."

Epilogue

SO NOW WHAT ARE you going to do?

There can be a more effective way to select team members for your team. Many leaders like Bob Paul have muddled along, rolling the dice that someone they have selected to join their team will be successful.

Is it important to you to add the same kind of rigor to your selection process that you expect in your accounting processes?

Are you willing to step back and look at your selection process through the eyes of the CEO's Advantage?

Are you willing to look at the gap between what you are currently doing now as a leader and what you need to be doing in order to make selection decisions with a level of confidence you have never felt before?

It is often a systematic approach to interviewing that differentiates the really good interviewer from one who is depending on luck for a good outcome.

There is an old Chinese proverb that says:

When you hear something, you will forget it.
When you see something, you will remember it.
But not until you do something, will you understand it.

To take your first step to more confident selection decisions, simply visit www.theceosadvantage.com.

Let's get started.

Stephen C. Moulton
Broomfield, Colorado
March, 2008

The Process

THE INTERVIEW USED BY most interviewers to select new employees is not reliable in predicting a candidate's potential for success on the job. That's reality.

Yet, in researching the processes that could truly and easily turn the advantage to you, the evidence is very strong that the use of the seven keys is very powerful and reliable.

Over the last twenty years or so, the following key academic researchers have conducted and published studies on at least one of the seven keys to what makes an effective employment interview and selection decision:

Michael A. Campion of Purdue University

Michael A. McDaniel of the University of Akron

Frank L. Schmidt of the University of Iowa

Stephan J. Motowidlo of the University of Florida

Allen I. Huffcutt of Bradley University

Neal Schmitt of Michigan State University

Thomas W. Dougherty University of Missouri, Columbia

Willi H. Wiesner of Concordia University, Montreal

Steven F. Cronshaw of University of Guelph, Ontario

and many others . . .

Here is a summary of the results.

1. **Clearly Define the Position Requirements.**

Taking the time to do a formal analysis of a position's requirements can make a huge difference. In one experiment, three groups were asked to select six competencies from a list of defined competencies and then put them in the order of importance.

Each of the groups made a prioritized list. Then they were asked to conduct a position analysis using a simple tool to rate a series of behaviors. The result was that the wing-it list and the list that resulted from the position analysis were not even close.

When asked which list was correct, the overwhelming response was that the position analysis effort was much more reflective of what was essential for success in the job. The reason was that when each of the groups selected from the list, they were not as objective as when they looked at specific behaviors.

A thorough job analysis, taking several days, is viewed by experts as the most preferred approach. Yet, an objective approach taking less than an hour can yield results almost as good and just as defensible.

The bottom line is that the best prediction achievable for structured interviews would be obtained where structured interview questions are based on a formal job analysis rather than a less systematic assessment of job requirements.

2. Create a Structured Job-Related Interview.

Structured interviews, if preceded by a thorough job analysis, can be developed to tap the many skill and ability areas required for the job. Structured interviews are more than twice as effective as unstructured interviews.

Creating a structured interview based on a job analysis takes the effectiveness to the next level, increases the reliability of results, and is far more defensible.

Why do structured interviews have higher levels of validity? One theory is that they are better at assessing other factors related to success on the job.

Simply speaking, two researchers found that the typical unstructured interview, conducted by an experienced interviewer, had a reliability of predicting job performance of about 15-30%.

They also found that a structured past-event interview, based on a job analysis and using rating guides, could be 87% reliable in predicting job performance.

3. Use Past-Event Interview Questions.

A large number of studies have shown that the use of experience-based interview questions (questions about how a candidate has handled specific situations in the past) that are job related produce the best results in predicting a candidate's potential for success in the job.

In addition, studies have shown that experience-based interviews had little impact on, and were equally valid for, subgroups (White, Black, Hispanic, male, and female).

Several things need to be done for past-event interviews to be effective:

- Get verifiable information from candidates, including who would have been aware of this event and where and when it took place.
- Make sure that the challenge the candidate faced, the action they took, and the result they got is clear.
- Also, seek contrary examples to get a balanced picture of the candidate.
- Use silence effectively to allow the candidate time to think.
- Take good notes. Try to write down as much of what the candidate says as possible. A team interview will help, but if you have an assistant who can take shorthand or clear notes, assign him or her to take notes as a backup.

4. Use a Team Interview.

Panel interviews were more valid than individual interviews.

So what is the big deal? The traditional interviews most managers conduct will not keep your company ahead of the power curve.

If you want to improve your ability to hire the right people for the right positions, structured panel interviews add a lot of value.

Use a team of two or three team members—no more— each participating in the interview at the same time. Using a team interview that is structured can have a number of benefits:

- Minimizing error and bias;
- Hearing the same information at the same time;
- The synergy of helping each other probe more effectively;
- Helping each other stay legal, and;
- Sharing note taking duties.

There *are* pitfalls in conducting team interviews. Overcoming them requires a conscious effort, especially at the executive level.

Effective interviewing is not an intuitive process and interviewers need to be trained to be *effective* interviewers.

Interviewers need to follow a structured process, asking specific questions based on specific examples of how the candidate has handled specific situations in the past.

Disagreement on candidate fit must be supported by specific, verifiable examples presented by the candidate rather than a gut feeling or impression.

Ask each interviewer to resist early judgment in the interview, gather the examples for each of the interview questions, and then rate the responses against the competencies.

5. **Control Your Biases and First Impressions.**

Most people feel they can read people well and that their first impression is all it takes to make a good hiring decision. Yet bias and error by interviewers is a key reason for interviewing failure.

Without the use of scientific tools and effective training, interviewers will often make hiring decisions based on "gut feelings" and intuition. Gut feelings and intuition should be used to make probing more effective.

In one study, researchers found that interviewers tended to spend their interviews confirming their first impressions of job applicants. Interviewers gathered little information about a candidate, and if the first impression was positive, they tended to spend much of their time with the candidate selling the company and giving job information.

Don't get trapped into making "trait interpretations," which, at the typical interview level, are a combination of gut feelings and pop psychology. Using words like *attractive, sharp,* and *confident* as descriptors for a candidate are unverifiable interpretations.

The concepts in this book are focused on an approach of gathering examples of a candidate's past experiences in a verifiable and objective manner.

6. Establish Rating Guides in Advance.

"I'll know it when I see it" has been a common refrain from senior executives as they have worked their way through the interview process. Yet, research from several sources suggests that establishing rating guides in advance is vital for a sound interview process and hiring decision.

You will note that the interview questions provided in the back of the book include behaviorally anchored ratings and a positive and negative rating guide.

The difference between an interview built on a job analysis that links the interview questions and the rating guides and one that doesn't is profound. Decreasing subjectivity and increasing objectivity are significant steps toward the scientific end of the selection spectrum.

When interviewers have rating guides and a way to consistently rate the responses of a candidate, the reliability of results goes way up. That results in the need for fewer interviews, since any one team of interviewers will get essentially the same results as any other team of interviewers.

7. Rate Candidates by Consensus.

The use of consensus rating has been demonstrated to result in levels of validity significantly higher than the other approaches.

Why? Some researchers believe that when interviewers use a consensus rating, they are accountable to their peers and, hence, are more accurate in their ratings. Consensus ratings offer the raters the opportunity to point out specific aspects of a candidate's responses.

The consensus rating plays a key role in getting the right candidate. When interviewers and raters know they will have to meet and be accountable to their reasons for the fit of the candidate, they become more objective and thorough in their interviewing efforts.

Wrapping It Up

USING A PROCESS TO select key leaders is important. The process laid out in this book is designed to address each of the seven keys outlined above. Using those keys will make hiring extraordinary leaders possible. It will also give you the tools you need to make hiring decisions with consistency and confidence.

Hiring the right team can have a huge positive impact on the organization's bottom line and, at the same time, can positively impact the working environment in a big way. Better decisions lead to better results. It's as simple as that. And the seven keys provide the CEO's Advantage to get you there.

Candidate Rating Form

Position Title: Chief Financial Officer   Candidate: _____

Interviewer: _____   Date: _____

Rating Anchors	Strong Evidence Candidate Lacks Competency	Some Evidence Candidate Lacks Competency	Some Evidence Candidate Has Competency	Strong Evidence Candidate Has Competency
Behavioral Competencies				
1. Leadership				
2. Integrity				
3. Trust and Respect				
4. Develop Relationships				
5. Team Building				
6. Strategic Perspective				
7. Concern for Quality				
8. Collaboration				
Technical Competencies				
1. Manage Accounting Function				
2. Financial Strategies And Plans				
3. Financial Modeling				
4. Budget Reporting				
5. Budget Decisions				
6. Secure Capital				

Recommended for Position: [   ] Yes   [   ] No

Reason:_____

Bob Paul's Structured Interview

(For a printable PDF of this interview go to
www.theceosadvantage.com/interview)

Leadership: Able to develop and inspire others to take personal responsibility; get factions with competing perspectives to learn from one another; integrate efforts and talents of team members; lead people past status quo to achieve new levels of excellence.

1. Leadership, it has been said, means getting people to do things because they want to. When have you been successful in stimulating others to take personal responsibility? How did you do it?

_____

_____

_____

_____

_____

_____

_____

_____

_____

_____

Positive – The candidate was able to excite others to take personal responsibility for projects or actions in order to grow or change.
Negative – The candidate held people accountable by forcing personal responsibility or using a carrot and stick approach.

2. Leadership often means disrupting comfort zones in order to lead people past the status quo and achieve new levels of excellence. Describe a time when you were able to do this.

_____

_____

_____

_____

_____

_____

_____

_____

Positive – The candidate was able to create a positive disequilibrium by asking questions or raising issues that lead to change.
Negative – The candidate took a simplistic approach to change or was more comfortable with maintaining stability.

Integrity: Able to demonstrate sound ethical behaviors; show consistency between words and actions; do what is right even when no one is watching; consistently comply with organizational values.

1. Some rules seem to be made to be broken. Share with me an example of when you did what was right even when no one was watching.

_____

_____

_____

_____

_____

_____

_____

_____

_____

_____

Positive – The candidate demonstrated a concerted effort to do what was right even when it would have been easier not to have done so.
Negative – The candidate was immature, regretted the choice, or felt that it could catch up to him/her.

2. To some companies, consistent compliance with organizational values and practices is important and to others, it doesn't seem to be as important. Tell me about a time when you decided to risk loosing something important in favor of living an organizational value.

_____

_____

_____

_____

_____

_____

_____

_____

_____

_____

Positive – The candidate's actions were consistent with the company standards and were an appropriate risk.
Negative – The candidate's actions were inconsistent with the company standards or were insignificant.

Trust and Respect: Able to build one-on-one relationships, incorporating trust and respect; deal with people in an open and honest manner; keep word and follow through on commitments; keep the dealings with organizations or individuals confidential.

1. Describe a situation in which you built trust and respect by keeping your word and fulfilling a commitment. What was the situation and what did you do?

_____

_____

_____

_____

_____

_____

_____

_____

_____

Positive – The candidate described a situation that required keeping a promise that was significant or difficult to keep.
Negative – The candidate may have acted inappropriately in order to be liked or was superficial.

2. Being honestly concerned about the needs and feelings of another can be the basis for building a one-on-one relationship, incorporating trust and respect. Describe a time when you have done that.

_____

_____

_____

_____

_____

_____

_____

_____

Positive – The candidate was considerate and empathetic in developing and maintaining a positive long-term relationship.
Negative – The candidate saw the relationship as a means to an end, professional expectation, or obligation.

Develop Relationships: Able to build credibility and rapport with others; relate with others, initiate the building of a cooperative relationship with others; demonstrate awareness of others' needs; use appropriate humor to ease tension, without putting others down.

1. Describe a situation in which you built a relationship by demonstrating awareness of someone's needs. What was the situation and what did you do?

_____

_____

_____

_____

_____

_____

_____

_____

_____

Positive – The candidate described a situation that was quite insightful and made a difference in building a relationship.
Negative – The candidate may have lacked insight, acted inappropriately in order to be liked, or was superficial.

2. Tell me about a work experience when you went out of your way to build credibility and rapport with others.

_____

_____

_____

_____

_____

_____

_____

_____

_____

Positive – The candidate related well with others and built credibility and rapport in a difficult situation.
Negative – The candidate was superficial, spent too much time glad-handing, and lacked credibility.

Team Building: Able to get factions with competing perspectives to learn from one another; use a positive approach to motivate others; integrate efforts and talents of team members; develop enthusiasm in peers or subordinates.

1. Team building is often a difficult thing to do. Describe a time when you were able to develop and promote a team effort by getting factions with competing perspectives to learn from one another. Be specific.

Positive – The candidate took a thoughtful approach to improving communication, developing roles/vision, or building trust and respect.
Negative – The candidate promoted a "we vs. they" mentality, was autocratic, or emphasized the task to be completed.

2. The best teams seem to be made up of members who have significantly different talents, skill levels, and responsibilities. Tell me about a time when you were able to integrate the efforts and talents of such a team.

_____

_____

_____

_____

_____

_____

_____

_____

_____

Positive – The candidate helped the team recognize how the various talents and efforts integrated and promoted learning from each other.
Negative – The candidate didn't make full use of the different talents and efforts, showed favorites, or was directive.

Strategic Perspective: Able to recognize the broad implications of issues; develop long-term strategies to enhance the organization's competitiveness; identify efforts that would have the greatest strategic impact; balance big picture concerns with day-to-day activities.

1. Give me an example of a time in which you recognized the broad implications of issues that management was focused on and what you did.

_____

_____

_____

_____

_____

_____

_____

_____

_____

Positive – The candidate shared a significant example that was being dealt with and anticipated future consequences.
Negative – The candidate was too theoretical, over-complicated, or cynical about the issues rather than helpful.

2. Getting things done and planning don't always go hand-in-hand. Tell me about a time when you were able to balance big picture concerns with day-to-day activities at a time when you were under pressure.

_____

_____

_____

_____

_____

_____

_____

_____

_____

Positive – The candidate was able to balance, integrate, and communicate practical short-term activities with big picture perspective.
Negative – The candidate described an intolerance of day-to-day details or a lack of long-term foresight.

Concern for Quality: Able to promote quality results in spite of other pressures; identify and remove barriers to quality; deliver quality results in tasks and assignments; develop and maintain a culture of quality.

1. When have you been most proud of your ability to take time to ensure quality results when you had a high-pressure deadline?

_____

_____

_____

_____

_____

_____

_____

_____

_____

Positive – The candidate resisted adjusting quality shortcuts and passing on inferior results that would have to be fixed later.
Negative – The candidate responded to pressure by taking shortcuts that may have negatively impacted quality results.

2. Individual or team performance can be negatively impacted by barriers in the work process. Tell me about a time when you made an extra effort to remove barriers on either yourself or someone else who was preventing quality results.

_____

_____

_____

_____

_____

_____

_____

_____

Positive – The candidate used a quality-systems approach to identify and resolve problems or barriers and effectively prevented problems.
Negative – The candidate took minimal extra effort to remove a barrier, was impulsive, or used inappropriate methods.

Collaboration: Able to share ideas and learn from others to build consensus; contribute information and skills to help others achieve results; develop a synergy of ideas and efforts with team members; partner with team members, customers, and vendors.

1. Share with me an example of when you developed a synergy of ideas and efforts with team members to promote a collaborative effort.

_____

_____

_____

_____

_____

_____

_____

_____

_____

Positive – The candidate helped to create a positive energy, provide new relevant ideas, control the agenda and time, or involve others.
Negative – The candidate was directive, used pressure to get results, or there was little synergy in integrating ideas that promoted collaboration.

2. Tell me about an experience when you were proud of the results you got partnering with team members, customers, or vendors in a collaborative effort.

_____

_____

_____

_____

_____

_____

_____

_____

Positive – The candidate related well with others and built credibility and rapport in a difficult situation that resulted in a positive collaborative effort.
Negative – The candidate lacked insight into how to partner with others and was more directive than collaborative.

Acknowledgements

FIRST AND FOREMOST, I want to thank my wife Gayle for her love, support, and patience these many years and to the rest of my family for their constant support.

I feel so thankful. I feel like I wrote this book with a hundred helpers, including some who are gone—several teachers, bosses, and others who are far away and connected to me only by memories. I feel I owe so many people thanks for the influence they have been on my life and my career.

I appreciate the efforts and encouragement of Don Hutton, Dave Angus, Paul Demetter, Robin Bradbury, and others who thought this book touched on an important issue in a way that would engage leaders.

I want to thank Melanie Mulhall for her wonderful editing efforts. Nick Zelinger for his help in the cover design and page layout to make the book look good. Jace Martin for his artistic photo efforts to make me look good.

Thanks to John Eggen for his book writing insights and Leslie Malin for her ongoing support.

Many thanks to a new friend, Mark Myers, an accountability partner who helped me keep on track and who proofed the final manuscript. Also many thanks to Elenore Bergstresser for her detailed proofing of the book as well.

Thanks to the team at Flatirons Publishing for their commitment to bring this together.

A special thanks to all of the CEOs and other executives I've worked with over the years for giving me insight into the challenges they face and the need they have for every *Advantage* they can get.

And most important, I thank my Heavenly Father for all that I have and for the talents He has granted me.

About the Author

STEPHEN MOULTON, SPHR is founder and president of Action Insight, a management consulting firm specializing in helping leaders in hospitals and hospital systems who struggle with hiring and keeping really good people. As a consultant, speaker, and software inventor, he has worked with healthcare executives across the country. Clients who have engaged his services include Lee Memorial Health System, Shands Healthcare, Columbus Regional Healthcare, Avera Sacred Heart Hospital, to name a few.

Stephen is a member of American College of Healthcare Executives, American Society for Human Resources Administration, and Society of Human Resource Management.

Stephen lives in the beautiful Boulder area of Colorado with his wife Gayle.

To learn more about Stephen and Action Insight, please visit www.actioninsight.com.

Six Ways to Bring
The CEO's Advantage
into Your Organization

Bob Paul's Structured Interview

Access a free printable full-sized PDF copy of Bob Paul's structured interview. This offer and the following web link, will only be available for a limited time. To access the interview go to:
www.theccosadvantage.com/bpinterview

The CEO's Advantage PowerPoint Presentation

Introduce and reinforce The CEO's Advantage into your organization with this complete and cost-effective presentation. All of the main concepts and ideas in the book are reinforced in this professionally produced, downloadable PowerPoint presentation with facilitator guide and notes. $99.95.
Download at www.theceosadvantage.com.

Keynote Presentation

Invite Stephen Moulton to inspire your team and help create greater success for your organization. Each presentation is designed to set a solid foundation for both organizational and personal success.

The CEO's Advantage Workshop

Facilitated by Stephen Moulton for up to six key executives. This four-hour workshop will expand and reinforce the principles of The CEO's Advantage, and each participant will learn how to implement each of the Seven Keys that can make a profound difference in his or her hiring decisions.

Action Interviewing Workshop

Facilitated by Stephen Moulton or a certified Action Insight instructor, this daylong program will expand the concepts of the CEO's Advantage across the organization.

It provides the tools and skills necessary for managers to make better hiring decisions and reduce turnover significantly.

ActionPlus Web-based-Software

Automate the process of position analysis and create a database of position profiles and structured behavioral-based interviews.

You can also check us out at **www.actioninsight.com** or call **866-439-2001**.